LIGHTHOUSE

FOUR COUNTRIES - ONE AIM

by

Martin Boyle

B & T Publications

PUBLISHED BY B & T PUBLICATIONS,

10 Orchard Way, Highfield, Southampton.

Hampshire SO17 1RD.

International Standard Book Number

ISBN 1-901043-02-9

Author's Acknowledgements

Historical narratives are either totally boring or fanatically interesting. To actually write about a subject of the past; especially when it relates so poignantly with the present and has a major role for the future, is a daunting task. Many details are often missed, with others assumed, or the authors licence used to fictitious effect to fill in the missing pieces. As the author of this publication, I set myself the task of researching deeper into a subject I believed I already knew a great deal about. However, if I published all of my findings, there would be a book that was so big and heavy, no-one could pick it up without mechanical means. Regrettably, there are bound to be snippets of information that have been left out, but what has been written, I believe is the closest to the facts that is credibly possible to portray.

To thank everyone who has assisted during my research and to put them in order of priority is impossible. All I can say is that this narrative has been like a jig-saw puzzle. Without all the pieces, it could not have been completed.

Martin Boyle

Contents   Page No.

Lighthouses or Pharos? 5
The Origins of Aids to Navigation 5
Seamarks 6
Ecclestiastical Lights 6
Order out of Chaos 7
Brotherhoods, Fraternities and Guilds 7
Trinity Houses 8
Trinity House at Leith 8
Trinity Houses of Hull and Newcastle 9
Combined Corporations 10
Mariner's Trust of Lord Crewe 10
Wales & the Merchant Venturers 10
The Forgotten Irish Sailors 11
Royal Charter from Henry VIII 11
The First Master 12
Constitution of Trinity House of Deptford 12
Elizabeth I - Charter for Beacons, Buoys & Ballastage 13
In the Event of War 15
Early Lighthouse Laws and Levies 15
Speculation and Conflict of Rights 16
Royal Priviledge and Favouritism 17
Conflict of Interest 18
Private Owners, Smugglers and Wreckers 18
Strange Events at Spurn Point 19
Cromwell and Pepys 20
Pilot Licensing 21
Patronage and Press Gangs 21
Affairs of Lighthouses in Ireland and Scotland 22
Ballast Board of Dublin 23
Slow Growth in Scotland 24
Commissioners of Irish & Northern Lights 25
Private Ownership and Slow Progress on the Isle of Man 26
Costly End to Private Ownership of Lights - England & Wales 27
Skerries - The Last Private Lighthouse 29
Triple Partnership v Officialdom 29
Trinity House of Deptford Properties 30
Lighthouse Builders - Eccentrics, Silk Merchants & Violin Makers 31
The Eddystone Influence 32
Difficult Access 32
Dangerous Locations 33
Lighthouse Engineers 33
Royal Connections 34
Reform of Light Dues 34
More About the Trinity Houses 34
International Lighthouse Authority 35
Lighthouse Keepers - End of and Era? 35
Services Today 37
Future Maritime Navigational Policy 39
Even with Modern Technology 39
Reference Sources 39
Acknowledgements of Copyrights used in this Publication 40
Notifications 40
Further Publications 44

Lighthouses
Four Countries - One Aim

Dover Castle circa A.D.53 (Photo by K. Trethewey)

**Special acknowledgement to Dr. K.R. Trethewey and the
Lighthouse Society of Great Britain for the invaluable help in the
production of this publication.**

Lighthouses or Pharos?

It can only be assumed when the first planned lighthouse was established as a maritime navigational aid. However, there are numerous references to fishing families who erected lights on poles or in cottage windows, to guide their men-folk back to safety. It goes without question that a bright light positioned in a high prominent location, will be easily seen. In turn this would provide a light that is readily distinguishable from other lights in the vicinity.

The first planned lighthouse is understood to be the majestic '*Pharos of Alexandria*' around 285 B.C. Although many historians believe the famous '*Colossus of Rhodes*'; erected in 300B.C. to be the original lighthouse, the '*Pharos*' was well documented. According to the '*Geographia Nubiensis*', the '*Pharos*' was '*100 statures of man, or 300 cubits, or 512 English feet* (156m).' The name pharos was not the actual tower, but the name of the small Island of Pharos on which it stood.[1]

Other nations use different terms. The Germans refer to a '*leuchtturme*' or light tower; the Spanish and Italians use '*phare*', with English speaking peoples calling them lighthouses. However, during the early days of the Lloyd's signalling stations, the lexicographers argued in vain that their towers were the only true lighthouses. But when considering either '*pharos*' or '*lighthouses*', they are in fact the same, because the word pharology means the study of things related to lighthouses.

In the grounds of Dover Castle, Kent, stands what is believed to be the first planned '*pharos*' in England. Although it has been altered over the past centuries, historical references put the construction of this structure during the reign of Emperor Claudius in A.D.53. It formed one of a pair of towers; the other built at Boulogne in France, during the reign of Emperor Caligula some forty years earlier. Although recorded as being used mainly for signalling towers, across the English Channel, it is well documented that they were employed as lighthouses for part of their history.

The Origins of Aids to Navigation

It is difficult for us as we enter the 21st century, to appreciate the problems faced by the mariner, in the days before the introduction of planned navigational aids. By the day it was beneficial to remain in sight of land; because with experience or good information of the location, it was possible to navigate by using prominent features. Also, early mariners associated white topped waves and swirling waters, with possible hidden rocks. However by night the mariner found he was better off braving the waves of the open ocean, which placed him far from the unseen submerged reefs and dark rocky outcrops. Unless ample time was available to avoid a danger, especially with vessels under sail, the consequences would prove disasterous.

'*Swinging the lead*' was the process used by sailors to check the depth of the water below a ship's keel. When a vessel was built a rope line was hung from the deck level to the line of the keel, with its length given in '*spans*'. This measurement was originally calculated to be the distance between the points of the thumb and the little finger, on a spread hand. When this measurement was known a knot was tied or spliced to represent the deck height, with a heavy lead weight attatched to the other end. Above the spliced knot further rope markers were fixed at distances of a fathom, or the maximum distance between a man's extended arms, or 6ft (1.83m). This method was considered to be the only safe means for checking the depth of water, but usually it was employed when dangers were expected. Major civilisations such as the Greeks, Phoenicians, Romans and Vikings, travelled great distances in uncharted waters and soon realised the benefits of navigational aids - seamarks by day and lights by night.

Seamarks

Seamarks have always been considered more important than lights. This is because in the early days of sail, reliable lights did not exist. Traditionally seamarks were clumps of trees, church steeples, prominent rock formations or any other obvious feature of the land that could readily be distinguished from the sea. The term '*seamarks*' later took on a meaning which referred to buoys, beacons and lights. Today the official recognition of a seamark is shown as lighthouses with their distinctive colours, or those which are noted in the Admiralty handbooks. A '*beacon*' conventionally came to mean a navigational aid for day use, which consisted of masts, pillars or other erections of brick, stone or timber. There is also an understandable mistake which has been associated with '*fire beacons*,' as a means for guiding the mariner. In fact this system was for the purpose to warn of an impending invasion. These fire beacons were erected as early as the 5th century, although during the 14th and 15th centuries, they were mostly situated from Land's End in Cornwall to the mouth of the Thames near London. As a fire was lit, so the next one was set ablaze, until the whole coastline showed a succession of warning lights.

However, records show the use of isolated fire beacons that were employed by the Hanseatic League around 1250-1550. By 1280, various groups of Rhineish merchants had formed a collective, in order to protect their common interests in sea-trade. Many of their foreign trade centres were situated in Brugge, Bergen and London. When one of the vessels was close to its port of destination, fire signals would be lit to guide it safely into harbour.

Currently, a seamark is defined as '*an artificial or natural object of easily recognisable shape or colour or both, situated in such a position that it maybe identified on a chart or related to a known navigational instruction.*' This was a good definition throughout seafaring history, although charts were not generally used until the early 16th century.

Between the 11th and 12th centuries, religious orders began documenting distinctive or prominent land-falls and seamarks. These became particularly useful during the era of the Crusades. From these early beginnings, ecclesiastical lists became known as '*rutters*' or '*sailing directions*'. Today the modern equivalent is considered to be the Admiralty List of Lights and Seamarks.

Ecclestiastical lights

From medieval times to the beginning of the 17th century, the safety of seamen, was a task which often fell to the caring people of the church. Indeed, the majority of early maritime lights were of ecclesiastical origin. One of the first recorded lights, established by a religious order in the British Isles, was at Hook Head in County Wexford; reputed to be the site where the monks of St. Dubhan established a fire beacon as early as the 5th century. Another report gives 810 as the date of establishment, but there is no doubt that the tower that exists there today is the oldest operational light in any of the four countries and dates from 1245.

It was reportedly built by the Warden and Chaplains of the Monastery of St.Savior Rendeuan. A lighthouse is said to have been built at Youghal in Ireland, around 1190 by Maurice Fitzgerald, who put it in the care of the nuns of St. Ann's convent which she endowed. In England the earliest known light; apart from the Dover pharos, was a harbour light at Winchelsea on the Kent coast erected about 1261.

Although the ecclesiastical orders may have tended the lights, not all were built by them. St. Catherines's oratory on the Isle of Wight, was erected by a rich merchant to stave of ex-communication by the Papal Church. The merchant, Walter de Godeton, purchased numerous barrels of wine from a local wrecking community at St. Catherine's. Despite the principle of '*Custom *and Descent'*; where salvage from shipwrecks was considered the lawful right of the people, the Pope considered this to be an act of plunder and sacrilege because the wine had been destined for the Church. As penance, Walter de Godeton was forced to build the St. Catherine's oratory; to provide a *'chaunting priest'* and to establish a *'light for the benefit of the mariners, to be lit every night for ever.'* From 1314 until dissolution of the Papal monasteries by Henry VIII in 1534, the descendants of Walter de Godeton kept the oratory lit. [2]

One of the most famous medieval lights in the British Isles, was exhibited from the top of St. Michael's Mount Church in Cornwall. This coalburning light was established around the middle of the 14th century, with the Church standing proudly on its island base, off the fishing port of Marazion.

It may seem strange that one of the last remaining ecclesiastical lights to be in operation, was in the North Devon coastal town of Ilfracombe. This particular light was exhibited from the Chapel of St. Nicholas, on Lantern Hill. Originally this light was introduced for the protection of fishermen, by the local priest, around the middle of the 13th century. Its purpose was to provide a marker for the treacherous Norte Stone and Rockham Shoals. When lit it was reported to be visible by shipping for up to 5 nautical miles and for its 650 year history, it was only extinguished during the first and second World wars.

Ecclesiastical lights were shown in Scotland, with the best known at Leith near Edinburgh from 1522. The last light erected by a religious order in Scotland, was in 1566 at Aberdeen. [6]

Order out of Chaos

Shipwrecks were both good and bad news. Bad for the sailors and their families, but good for the people that lived nearby and could benefit from salvage of the cargoes. Such windfalls often meant the difference between comfort and despair in lean times. Once the mariner came to depend upon certain lights being shown, it was only a matter of time before unscrupulous rogues showed false lights to lure ships onto the deadly rocks. The Cornish coasts, in particular, hold many secrets of wreckers and their deadly games.

One well documented North Cornwall wrecker and smuggler, tied a lantern to his donkeys tail. As the animal walked around it gave an old recognition signal, similar to a waving light. This particular signal was often used by fishermen and those mariners who associated the light as to mean a safe haven. During this heartless time, the Cornish wreckers would more often salvage the ship's cargo, before aiding a stricken mariner. In many cases they murdered the surviving seaman, to ensure they were unable to lay claim to the right of salvage. In the 14th century, piracy at the Bell Rock in Scotland, is the focus of a tale in which a warning bell was established on this dangerous outcrop by the Abbot of Aberbrothock. A notorious pirate removed the bell in order to further his own evil ends. However, it is said that a year later he perished, when his ship was wrecked on the same rock. [3]

Brotherhoods, Fraternities and Guilds.

Dangers faced by seamen throughout history have led to a kindred spirit of compassion and charity rarely matched in other walks of life. From earliest times they formed into groups and associations, to look after the interests of their brothers of the sea and their families. No matter how small or large, *'Brotherhoods'*, *'Fraternities'* or *'Guilds'* arose and developed into recognisable associations. These old Guilds were religious in character and designed for mutual benefit of their members. Help was given to the poor, the aged or the sick and to their dependants.

Some Guilds were more successful than others and, as history passed, the large ones became well established around mainland Britain. In Deptford, at the Thames estuary, was created the medieval '*Guild of Mariners*', from which stemmed the Corporation of Trinity House.

Deptford was originally the oldest business centre where the trading of the Port of London occurred. For centuries Deptford held the monopoly of all sea-trade for the region, until around the beginning of the 15th century when the River Thames was dredged. From this time shipping was able to navigate further up the river and closer to the City of London. Within a few years after the dredging had been completed, Deptford fell into disuse.

There are no known records which relate to the '*Guild of Mariners*'; although various historical documents give reference to its existence, but there are theories which provide an insight to its creation. The first indication pertains to a religious order, that existed at the time of King Alfred (871-899). The second suggests that the fraternity was founded by the Archbishop of Canterbury, Stephen Langton (1207-1228), during the reign of King John. The records state that the '*Guild*' or '*Fraternity*' was composed of: '*godley disposed men who for the actual suppression of evil disposed persons bringing ships to destruction by the showing forth of false beacons do bind themselves together in the love of the Lord Christ in the name of the Masters and Fellows of Trinity Guild, to succour from the dangers of the sea all who are beset upon the coasts of England to feed them unhungered and athirst, to bind up their wounds and to build and light proper beacons for the guidance of mariners.*'

Trinity Houses

There were other Societies of Mariners known as Trinity Houses, at Dover, Dundee, Hull, Leith and Scarborough. These '*Guilds*' all evolved in slightly different ways and had varying degrees of authority. The Trinity House at Dover, for example, was a '*Court of Loadsmanage.*' With a loadsman being a pilot, Dover was therefore responsible for all the pilotage; whether the Kings Navy or Merchant vessels, which was authorised by a Commission from the Lord Warden of the Cinque Ports. However, this Commission appears to have taken the form of a localised agreement. From the papers of John Whormby; an 18th century historian and also a secretary for the Trinity House of Deptford he states: '*the Trinity House of Dover had no Grants from the Crown and the Lord Warden of the Cinque Ports had no Patents relative to that department.*' [4]

Dover was the centre for '*loadsmange*' for many years. However, this came to an end when the work was consolidated with the pilotage of the Trinity House of Deptford. This followed an Act of Parliament in 1853. When this change occurred, the Trinity house of Dover faded out of existence.

Along with lighthouses, buoys, beacons and ballastage, pilotage has consistently been one of the main roles associated with the various Trinity Houses.

Trinity House of Leith

In Scotland, the Trinity House of Leith owed its conception to the charitable spirit of the seafaring men of the Port, who were aware that their fortunes were subject to '*hourly hazards and the fear of extreme poverty and beggary*'. They resolved to impose a levy of '*twelve pennies, Scots,*' on every ton of merchandise, which was loaded or unloaded from Scottish ships at the Port of Leith. This levy would be for the relief of the poor, aged and infirmed in Leith. It is uncertain when this resolution was made or when the first collection of this levy called the '*Prime Gilt*' was imposed, but indications suggest it to stem from 1380. On 10th May 1566 Mary Queen of Scots granted a precept under the Privy Seal, which ratified and confirmed the gift, foundation and erection of a hospital and the Prime Gilt.

In its Charter, granted to the House in 1797 by George III, it states that the Fraternity had '*tended to promote, increase and further commerce and navigation*' in the British Isles and chiefly in Scotland and the Port of Leith. None of the records that relate to this Fraternity of Masters and Mariners, shows any direct involvement with the political aspects of maritime affairs. However, it is clear that as seamen they were anxious for the safety of their ships and crews. It is worthy of note, that although they had no formal powers, their services were often called upon in the capacity of consultants.

The harbour of Leith belonged to the town of Edinburgh, with its management and maintenance the responsibility of its Town Council. The lights in the Firth of Forth were maintained by their owners, who imposed a duty on ships entering the port of Leith for their upkeep.

During 1860 the '*Prime Gilt*' generated an annual income of '*£1984.17s.7d.*' But an Act of Parliament the following year, saw this levy abolished. This more or less permanent income, for the Trinity House of Leith, saw a dramatic reduction. Without suitable funding this Fraternity found it hard to remain in existence. [3]

Trinity Houses of Hull and Newcastle

The activities of the Trinity House of Hull, was mainly pilotage and as an agent for the Lord High Admiral for the collection of ballastage dues. The charitable interests of this Fraternity, ran closely with the Trinity House of Deptford. Acknowledgement of its humanitarian work, was given with the Henry VIII Charter, issued on the 7th November 1541.

About five years earlier, on the 5th October 1536, Henry VIII had awarded another Charter, which formed the Corporation of Trinity House at Newcastle. Along with this Royal Approval, was issued a Letter-Patent which allowed for the erection of two towers; one on either side of the Tyne Estuary. By day these structures were intended as leading markers for shipping and at night lit with a coal or wood burning fire. Local Tynemouth Parish records show that this project was completed in 1540, with a light levy charged for its upkeep of '*two pence sterling for English ships and four pence for foreign vessels.*' Although these rudimentary lights served a local purpose, they were not considered to be for shipping in general.

It would not be until about 1594, during the reign of Elizabeth I, that the Trinity House of Newcastle would be involved with the establishment of England's second official lighthouse. This followed numerous requests to the Corporation of Trinity House of Deptford, to instigate the siting of a lighthouse at Tynemouth.

However, with the obvious shortage of suitable funds for such a project, it was left to the Trinity House of Newcastle to get the backing of the local council. Tynemouth Castle was considered the best location which took away the need for a purpose made lighthouse. Once activated the Mayor and Aldermen of Newcastle brought pressure to bear for the establishment of this light. However, Queen Elizabeth was concerned that a light could easily be used as a guide by her enemies at a time of war.

To overcome the objection, the Mayor and his Aldermen suggested that the management of the light be vested with the Earl of Northumberland. Not only was the Earl a valued member of the Queen's Privy Council, but the Captain of Tynemouth Castle. The project was given the Queen's Royal approval, with a Letter-Patent which stated that '*a coal burning light shall be shown every night during the night season.*' [5]

Combined Corporations

Although the various Trinity Houses were initially created for charitable purposes, as time progressed they soon became associated more with lighthouses, which would provide a greater degree of safety for the mariner. Prior to the middle of the 19th century, these Houses played a major role in influencing the plans of private lighthouse speculators. However, with legislation being predominantly directed towards London and the Trinity House of Deptford; which necessitated the other Houses having to obtain its sanction for any lighthouse projects, progression to only one Trinity House was inevitable. In 1836 this was the final outcome, with the Headquarters on Tower Hill becoming known as '*The Trinity House*'.

Mariner's Trust of Lord Crewe

Apart from the recognisable charitable institutions, there were various private individuals who made provisions for distressed seafarers. One in particular was Lord Crewe, the owner of Bamburgh Castle in Northumberland.

The location of Bamburgh Castle, is the mainland town which covers the Farne Islands and the Longstone Reef. Its position is about 20 miles from the border of Scotland, which has placed it in the chronicles of English and local history. As well as being fought over by the Romans, it has been sacked by the Scots, been the scene for an invasion by the Danes and strongly battled for by the medieval Kings of Mercia and Northumbria.

Bamburgh has been witness to some of the most tragic shipping incidents with the 18th centuary producing heartless acts of barbaric wrecking by the local inhabitants. However, on the death of Lord Crewe, he bequeathed that most of the money derived from his tenants and estates, had to be used for establishing a charitable school and a Distressed Seaman's Trust. Dr. John Sharpe, the administrating executor for the Trust, set up the school in part of the Castle ruins and on its ramparts he sited fog bells and guns to warn passing shipping during heavy weather. He also paid two horsemen to patrol the shores around Bamburgh during gales or storms, to look out for ships in distress. Even one of the first lifeboat stations was established in the village, with many of the local people being paid to assist in launching the heavy boat.

By the early 19th century navigational handbooks or rutters stated that: '*dead bodies cast upon the shore are decently buried gratis.*' These sailing directions also informed the mariner: '*a weeks victuals and lodgings and fresh clothes to be given to distressed seafarers.*' It is also understood that funds were made available for getting these people back to their homes. Dr. Sharpe approached a more civilised attitude towards wrecking and encouraged the local people to report any shipwreck, for which a premium reward was paid. These inhabitants soon realised that they could get more money from reporting a ship than from the sale of its salvaged cargo. When any wreck cargo was later sold, a percentage of the sale went to the Distressed Seaman's Trust.

Wales & the Merchant Venturers

Very little has been recorded which refers to charitable interests for the mariner, which can be associated with Wales. However there are various records, held in the Bristol Record Office, which relate to Bristol, Cardiff, Swansea, Milford Haven and Holyhead, that refer to the Honourable Society of Merchant Venturers. This Society was composed of Shipowners, Masters and Merchants, who had formed themselves into a collective in order to protect their interests, which were predominantly with the profitable coastal sea-trade.

During the middle of the 18th century, this Society set up its headquarters near to the rapidly expanding Port of Bristol. One of the Society's policies, was to consider the seamen who crewed their vessels. Suitably qualified and experienced sailors were hard to find, this shortage of labour being brought on by the colossal volume of sea trade.

In many cases seamen were taken on just to cover one voyage from port to port, simply because the ship would only have one cargo planned, with her Master having to look for another for the return trip. In order to ensure the best crews were always available, the Merchant Venturers set aside a premium, normally deducted from the seaman's pay, as charitable funds for their dependents. This action was soon recognised by the majority of the Shipowners and Merchants from Bristol to Holyhead, with most of the cargoes only being carried by those ships involved with the collective. At one time this Society was so powerful, even the owners of private lighthouses, such as Flatholm, Smalls, St. Ann's Head and the Skerries, allowed special rates of light levies.

In later years the involvement of Unions became the dominant force, which set aside charitable funds for its members. This was particularly noticeable with vessels which carried coal or iron ore from the various Welsh ports.

The Forgotten Irish Sailors

The hard working, yet just as hard living Irish seamen, did little to encourage any Charitable Societies to be formed. These men clearly felt that if they could not work for a living they were not worth anything. In some cases this pride over shadowed reality, with the numerous lean times and tragic shipping disasters; that involved the Irish sailor, having no Charitable means of support.

With the core of the Irish population being predominantly under the religious belief of the Papal Order, charitable concerns were normally administered by the Church. Only a few Seamen's Missions were originally established around the Ports of Belfast and Dublin and these were of religious origin. The numbers of Irish shipowners and Masters were low, with the majority of the vessels belonging to English ports such as Liverpool. It was therefore practically impossible to impose of levy, which could be used for distressed seamen. All the money that was obtained from shipping was taken by the respective Harbour Authorities, who were not disposed into providing any charitable interest. It is only fair to say, that up to 1922, the British attitude had always looked upon the Emerald Isle as an annex for England.

Even with the dramatic expansion of the major Irish ports, no organisation such as the Trinity Houses was ever formed. Any funding for the various Seaman's Missions therefore depended on wills, donations and in some cases a certain percentage of the sale of salvaged cargoes. There are records which show the involvement of the Church, with its claim to '*its Right of Salvage*'. This related to any cargo washed ashore or recovered along the coastal areas of a particular diocese.

Royal Charter from Henry VIII

Prior to the formal recognition of lighthouses as a necessary means of maritime navigation, the '*Respectable Company of Mariners, in the College of Deptford*' had petitioned Henry VIII, because of lack of suitably qualified mariners who could pilot the '*King's ships*'. On the 19th March 1513, these Master Mariners presented their petition at Canterbury, where it was accepted by the Lords of the Privy Council. In turn it was formally presented to Henry VIII.

This was a very long petition; signed by the '*Respectable Company of Mariners*' and numerous Masters of the Kings Navy, was instigated following Henry VIII deciding that Deptford would be a site for one of his major dockyards. These memorialists stated on the petition that many of the young men who assisted in pilotage along the River Thames, were inexperienced and easily tempted into making money from wrecking. They also stated that these men were: '*unwilling to take the labour and adventure of learning the shipman's craft of the high seas*'. Further more, there could be grave consequences if this practise continued as it made it dangerous to allow: '*foreigners, including Scots, Flemings and French, the opportunity to learn the secret of the King's streams.*' Henry VIII agreed with the content of the petition and commanded his Privy Council to implement a Royal Patent to be drawn up and a Charter of Royal Approval with the King's Great Seal to be issued , which would form the College of Deptford into a '*Perpetual Corporation.*' The '*Respectable Company of Mariners*' title was recorded on the Charter as the: '*Master, Wardens and Assistants of the Guild or Fraternitie of the most glorious and blessed Trinity and saint Clement* (Patron Saint of Mariners) *in the parish Church of Deptford Stronde, in the County of Kent.*' The Official awarding of the Royal Charter to Trinity House was on the 20th May 1514. The main basis of its authority was stated as being a Royal Licence to the '*Master's, Rules and Mariners of the King's Navy.*' It is clear from other documents held in the Public Record Office in London, that the Navy Board was not happy with the outcome of the Charter, because it meant that only those men '*suitably qualified*' and authorised by Trinity House, were allowed to pilot the King's ships into harbour anywhere in England. [7]

The First Master

The Charter was accepted from Henry VIII by Sir Thomas Spert, '*Comptroller of the Navy*' and the Master of the then prestigious man-o-war, the '*Henri Grace A Dieu*', the King's flag ship, affectionately known as the '*Great Harry.*' This ship carried guns in the waist, in addition to those on the fore and aft castle, which made it the most powerful ship afloat. Sir Thomas Spert was the first person to hold the coveted title of Master of Trinity House who became the longest continual holder of this position [1514-1541]. After this period, the constitution was changed, with all Elders or Masters to hold their position for only three years, after which time they had to stand down or be re-elected by the Trinity Court of Brethren.

Apart from the main contents of the 1514 Charter, one item was wrongly worded. Although a clause made the members of Trinity House excempt from all land-based military services; including jury service, they were required to serve the Crown at sea in times of war. Members could; in theory at least, be press-ganged into Naval service. Many years would pass before this matter was addressed and changed. [8]

Constitution of Trinity House of Deptford

From its first constitution, the number of the Court at Trinity House was one Master, four Wardens and eight Assistants, a total of 13. This number has strong connotations with the Holy Trinity, literally '*three in one*'. The composition of the court was raised by the James I Charter of 1604 from 13 to 31; a number still retaining the digits one and three, the extra 18 being called Elder Brethren. Although members had always been known as Brethren; derived from the old Brotherhoods, this Charter was the first to refer to Elder and Younger Brethren, respective terms which survive today. The Younger Brethren were admitted at the pleasure of the Trinity Court, but with no official function except for casting their vote during the election of the Master or Wardens. [8]

One of the main understandings which applied to any of the Brethren, was their close association with the sea. As Master Mariners or actual Shipowners in many cases, it placed them in the position of being well versed in the problems of maritime matters.

Elizabeth I
Charter for Beacons, Buoys and Ballastage

The authority of Trinity House of Deptford became frustrated, when the Brethren wanted to put forward an official register of all British seamarks. Numerous landowners petitioned Queen Elizabeth, because the proposed Act encompassed tall trees, barns, coastal farm houses and various prominent land-marks which they believed should not be classed as a navigational aid.

Even the Church objected, when it was noted that spires and towers were also included. More importantly the Act would give the Corporation the power to impose fines if any of these seamarks were removed without its permission. The final objection came from the owners of the Cinque ports who felt the income from their seamark levies would be seriously eroded, if the Corporation became the major beneficiary of these dues. Even with all these seemingly valid objections, the Act was passed by Queen Elizabeth and her Privy Council in 1566. From this time, Trinity House was officially recognised as the Custodian of all British Seamarks. [9]

Included in the Act, it is stated that the erection of any new seamarks or lights could be built by Trinity House, but these projects had to be self-financing and not funded from the Privy Purse. To make this possible a major hurdle had to be overcome and that was the involvement of the Lord High Admiral. In his capacity he already had a Royal Patent which allowed him to collect the levies from shipping, that used various buoys or beacons for navigation. He also held the rights for the ballastage, mainly from the Thames.

To add to the confused situation, ship Masters closely guarded their sea charts and rutters, which made it necessary for Trinity House to prove they actually used these land-based seamarks to navigate. Without this proof no levy could be imposed. Although Trinity House sent a succession of petitions to the Lords of the Privy Council, asking them to resolve problems relating to the Lord High Admirals Patent, his authority was upheld and the memorials rejected.

Dealings in ballast were two fold. Firstly the dredging up of sand and shingle from the river bed to keep the channels and wharfages clear and secondly the supplying of gravel to ships, for steading them when light or unladen. Originally ballastage was officially *'gravel, sand soil of the Thames'* which the operator was to *'land and lay on shore upon any of our waste ground'*; it was also forbidden to *'sell, vend, give or utter any gravel, sand or soil without a license.'* These licences were held by recognised ballast owners although in reality they were only sub-contractors. The only way that the vessels in the Thames; His Majesty's as well as others, could obtain their shingle or gravel was through these owners. Therefore the most profitable way was to make the ballastage a monopoly.

Ballastage became one of the first monopolies in the British Isles, which was given as a Royal Patent and privilege to the Lord High Admirals of England. In turn these Lords sub-let the rights of ballastage, with the first Patent being issued to the Earl of Surrey. In 1517 the Earl sub-let the rights of ballasting ships, to Thomas Spert, at an annual rental of £10. In 1541 there was further sub-rentals by the Lord High Admiral, Earl Russell, to various persons in respect of Rotherhithe and Limestone. This arrangement continued with successive Lord High Admirals.

As the Corporation's influence grew its achievements were finally rewarded on the 13th January 1573, when Trinity House was granted its Coat-of-Arms with the motto, '*Trinitas in Unitate.*' The Brethren were led to believe that the office of the Lord High Admiral would be forced to surrender the rights to collect the shipping levies in favour of the Corporation. Instead the Coat-of-Arms was all that was issued, formally granted by Elizabeth I and presented by Sir Gilbert Dethicke, recorded on the documents as the '*Knight of the Garter, Principal King of Arms and Chief Officer of Arms for the most honourable Order of the Garter*'.

On the 8th July 1578, the position of Lord High Admiral was conferred on Lord Charles Howard, Baron of Effingham. His appointment led the Elder Brethren of Trinity House to believe that he would finally address the matter of the ballastage and beaconage levies. Although much speculation has been made as to the true facts relating to this period, it is understood from Public Record sources that Lord Charles greatly favoured the administration and management arrangements which had been set up by Trinity House. However, when the Lords of the Privy Council were informed of the proposed transference of the ballastage Patent, they refused to allow any changes to proceed because it would harm the Privy Purse at that particular time.

A break through came on the 27th May 1594, when Queen Elizabeth commanded Lord Howard to surrender his ballastage and beaconage rights to the Crown. The main reason for this intervention, was due to the confused system of collecting the ballastage levy. Firstly the monopoly had caused the sub-letting of the ballast to run out of control, with the level of dues being charged to Masters and Shipowners exceptionally high. In turn this had generated numerous complaints and petitions from angry shipowners, who rightly felt the inflated levies were becoming an unwarranted burden. More importantly, the fees that the Ballast Agents were deducting for their services, had seriously eroded the returns to the Royal Treasury. Obviously, the Queen could not administer the ballastage and beaconage personally, so she was advised by her Privy Council, to award the rights to Trinity House. It was recorded as being stated, that the Queen felt that the Corporation was the best and most deserving organisation to be given this important charge. Part of the 1594 Charter, which confers this authority on to Trinity House reads:

'*Whereas . . Charles, Lord Howard . . Baron of Effingham, and our great Admiral of England, hath . . absolutely surrendered . . the lastage and ballastage . . of all . . ships . . . in or upon the river of the Thames, betwixt Our City of London and the main sea . . and all his lawful right . . which he hath . . . by virtue of the said office of Great Admiral of England . . We will be pleased to give and confirm the premises unto the Master, Wardens and Assistants of the Trinity House of Deptford-Strond, in Our County of Kent.*'

On the 11th of June 1594, the new Charter was issued to Trinity House by William Brench, on behalf of Queen Elizabeth I.

'*And whereas he* (Admiral Howard*) hath . . . surrendered . . . all his rights. . . in . . erecting . . any beacons, buoys, marks and signs for the sea . . it is in and by Our Statute or Act of Parliament made in the eighth year of Our reign, specially and expressly ordained and enacted, that the said Master, Wardens and Assistants of the Trinity House of Deptford - Strond . . might lawfully . . at their cost and charges, make , erect and set up, such and so many beacons and signs for the sea, in such places . . as to them shall seem most meet , needful and requisite, whereby dangers may be avoided and escaped, and ships the better come to their ports without peril*'.

Trinity House of Deptford were now fully recognised as the '*Superintendents of All Seamarks*', with the only authority in the British Isles to collect the dues for beaconage and ballastage. The Act also commanded that if any seamarks were destroyed or removed, beacons and prominent signs for the sea, had to be erected in their place. Notably, lights or lighthouses were not mentioned in this draught. This Act further stated, that none of the recognised or accidental seamarks already in use, should be cut down or removed by the owners or their agents, without the permission of the Elder Brothers of Trinity House of Deptford. If this occurred, a fine could be imposed of *'one hundred pounds sterling'* and if the owner was not worth that sum, *'he should be convicted of outlawry'*.

In the Event of War

One of the least known roles of Trinity House of Deptford, was its duty under the Henry VIII Charter, to raise local militia when the threat of war arose. During the latter part of the 16th century, Trinity House was put on a war footing, when Elizabeth I became concerned about the rising threat of a Spanish invasion. Captain Robert Salmon (*Master of the Corporation 1588-9*), wrote to Lord Burghley (*one of the Queen's advisors*) and informed him that it was possible for 30 ships to be fitted out in four days. These would then be ready to sail for the use of the Lord High Admiral. A few days later, Lord Henry Seymour, the Lord High Admiral, ordered Captain Salmon to *'go with his galley and make ready to guard the mouth of the Thames'*. A former master for the Corporation, Captain William Borough (1585), sent a chart of the Thames and Medway to Lord Seymour, with a letter that stated *'30 or 40 good ships would be sent from Flushing, to assist the good Lord.'*

It is not recorded whether these ships were ever used for their intended purpose by Lord Seymour, but in 1797, during the mutiny at Nore, the Elders of Trinity House of Deptford, were ordered by the Lord High Admiral, to remove or destroy all the beacons and buoys along the River Thames. This action effectively stopped the mutineers from being able to navigate to the open waters of the English Channel.

There is only one recorded time in the history of the Corporation, that it has armed its ships for war. In 1803, it formed the Trinity House Volunteer Artillery Force, which was used to blockade the Thames at Lower Hope, as a defence against a threatened French invasion.

War was often used as an excuse for not establishing lighthouses around the English coastline. Both Elizabeth I and James I rejected numerous petitions for suitable lights, on the grounds that lighthouses would assist their enemies at a time of war.

Since the establishing of Trinity House of Deptford as a Corporation, it has only extinguished its lights on three occasions. The first time was during the Dutch Wars(1665-7), when Charles II and his Parliament, insisted that all beacons, buoys be removed from the Thames and the lights to be extinguished along the English coast. Ironically, more of the English fleet were sunk by this action, than by the Dutch Navy. However, during the first and second World Wars, Trinity House was ordered by Parliament to extinguish all lights. The only time they were allowed to be relit, was with the permission of the Admiralty for the use of passing Allied shipping. Even then Trinity House was only permitted to exhibit its lights at half power.

Early Lighthouse Laws and Levies

It is important that people should have spotted a way to make money from the ownership of lighthouses. Land-owners and speculators realised that if a light was provided, then those who used it for a commercial reason, should be made to pay for it.

Lighthouses soon became big business; around the reign of James I, but

15

not all of these entrepreneurs had honourable motives. To make any charge on Shipowners for the upkeep of the light, it was necessary to obtain a Royal Patent. Authority for private individuals to collect a levy from shipping, for a light, dates back to the 13th century when Henry II (1216-1272) issued the first Royal Patent.

This Patent was issued in 1261, to the Barons of the Cinque Port of Winchelsea, which entitled them to levy '*by compulsory means, two pence*' from every ship that entered the Port. With Royal Patents considered to be the ultimate permission given by the reigning monarch, under the '*Divine Right of Kings*', it was a treasonable offence to challenge this authority. From this early beginning, the entire principal of taxation known as '*Light Dues*', has been the system operated from this time, right up to the present day.

Speculation and Conflict of Rights.

The first recorded petition for a lighthouse from a private individual, was made in 1580 by a Gawen Smith. His proposal to Elizabeth I requested the authority to erect a light on the treacherous Goodwin sands, off the Kent coast. The Queen rejected this petition, because she considered the application was solely for financial gain and not for the well being of the mariner. It would appear from the contemporary documents of the House of Lords, that the Master of Trinity House of Deptford, Henry Church, objected to the Smith proposals, because of his known association with the wrecking communities. [10]

In 1612, Sir Edward Howard exploited his position in the court of James I and sponsored a petition for a lighthouse at Dungeness. A share of the profits from the proposed business venture, was offered to Sir Edward Howard, by the petitioner Hugh Bullock and his partner. The Elders of Trinity House of Deptford, objected to the petitioner but James I ignored the opposition and issued a Patent. Trinity House complained to the Attorney general, Sit Henry Yelverton and stated that the Patent was in breach of their Charter from Elizabeth I. [11]

It would not be until five years later, in 1617, that a letter relating to the Dungeness Patent, was sent to Trinity House by the Attorney General. His letter acknowledged the Corporation's Charter, which had given the right to erect all beacons and signs, but not the exclusive authority which was vested in the King. He wrote: '*his Majesty is not restrained to provide them* (Patents for Lights), *according to his Regal power and Justice for the safety of his subjects.*' [12]

When Hugh Bullock received his Dungeness Patent, the area of land around the lighthouse, was rent free for 50 years. He was also given the right to collect a compulsory levy of '*one penny sterling per tun, from every English ship*', for the upkeep of the light. However, James I reduced the levy to '*half a penny per tun*', after numerous shipowners complained that the light was badly maintained. Records of this period do show that during the time that Hugh Bullock exhibited his Dungeness light, the number of ships wrecked along this treacherous section of coast was dramatically reduced.

Amongst the other private individuals who became lighthouse owners, was Sir John Clayton. He obtained a comprehensive Patent for no less than five sites, but because he boasted to the Lords of the Privy Council, that 500 shipowners and merchants had promised to voluntarily contribute to their upkeep, his Patent was issued with no compulsory levy order. Because of this only two of his lighthouse were ever lit, with these sited at Corton. The remaining towers at the Farne Islands, Flamborough Head and Foulness, never exhibited a light. On Admiralty charts of this period, these were shown as '*lighthouses that hath no lights.*' The annual rent which Sir John Clayton had to pay to the Crown, as part of his Patent, was £20 for a period of 60 years.

Royal Privilege and Favouritism

Under its Royal Charter, Trinity House of Deptford held the exclusive rights to all seamarks and was expected by its *'Perpetual Patent'* to organise a uniform system of navigational lights. But during the early 17th century this failed to materialise with many of the lights being totally inadequate. The majority of the problems associated with these early lighthouses, stemmed from the practice of *'Royal Favourites'*. With the power vested solely with the monarch and not by the Parliamentary system that we know today, it was common for certain members of the Royal Court to capitalise on their favoured positions. Anyone who wished to obtain a lighthouse Patent would need to watch for the right time, when the King was in a good mood. In some cases, financial rewards placed into the *'Right Pockets'* swayed the result of a petition. [8]

To add to the problems of Trinity House, many of the members of the Royal Court, were jealous of the Corporations large profits from ballastage and the beaconage levies, which they considered to be excessive for the minimal work it entailed. James I was advised to instigate an investigation into the powers of Trinity House Deptford, with the view of ensuring that more funds were available for the *'Privy Purse'*. One of the first actions by James I, was the process of favouring private lighthouse ownership. However, various records of this period clearly show that this was not necessarily for the *'Royal Treasury'*, but more for his own *'Royal Pocket'*.

The Elder Brothers of Trinity House objected to the actions of the Privy Council and reminded these Lords, that with all due respect to the King, the Corporation had exclusive rights for these seamarks. A compromise was reached whereby James I gave the Corporation the authority to erect lighthouses, but stated that it would have to apply to the King for a Patent on each occasion. This allowed the King the right to issue, at his own discretion, Patents for lighthouses in virtue of common law and his *'Divine Right'* as the reigning monarch. Trinity House wrongly assumed from this agreement, that when it applied for a lighthouse Patent, one would be issued as a mere formality. In fact, this was not the to be the case. [14]

This action by James I clearly went against both the spirit and the letter of the Elizabeth I Charter, for now the Sovereign could grant leases or sell land to private speculators. Within a few years every rock, island or stretch of potential coastline, was being examined by the *'Favourites of the Royal Court'*, for possible lucrative lighthouse Patents. In turn this made it impossible; in many cases, for Trinity House to obtain Patents, because the normal speed of permission was related to the size of the financial return to the King.

Trinity House still had the power to oppose any proposed project and on several occasions its objections were upheld. However, indications show that those which were refused, had not been particularly favoured by the King and that Trinity House was being used as an excuse for the rejection of a petition. Other projects were allowed to proceed but with a clause in the Patent, which only allowed for the voluntary collection of the light dues. The apparent confused system for these early lighthouse Patents, brought the weight of the Shipowners behind the Corporation, who were more in favour of a uniform rate of light dues. Although numerous Shipowners and Merchants had backed the original petitions, the majority of these did everything they could to avoid paying any contribution to the lights.

In some cases the lighthouse owners way laid ships as they passed their lights and forced the Masters to pay the dues before they were allowed to continue their voyage. This action brought numerous complaints to the attention of the Privy Council, who, in some cases, revoked the lighthouse Patent. Other complaints from Shipowners and Masters, stated that the lights were poorly managed, some indistinguishable from others along the coast and in some cases not lit at all. Trinity House was quick to respond by backing the Shipowners objections. With so many different rates being charged and their calculations based upon varying methods to define the word 'ton', the Corporation lobbied the Privy Council for the introduction of a uniform standard. Trinity House suggested the fairest calculation should be based upon 'tuns' and not 'tons'. With most of the merchant vessels carrying barrels which contained the cargoes, the Corporation obtained the backing of the majority of the Shipowners and Masters, to base the levies on 'tuns'. This term was well known during this period, to mean a cask of wine containing approximately 252 gallons - (1152 lts). All that was needed was the total number of 'tuns' that a vessel could carry, multiplied by the rate given in the Patent.

Conflict of interest

In 1617 Royal Privilege and 'politics' came into conflict when Trinity House instructed two Elder Brethren, Captains Norreys and Gere, to erect a lighthouse at Winterton. By that summer, the Winterton tower was completed with authority granted by the Privy Council of James I. But while Norreys and Gere were building the Winterton lighthouse, Sir William Erskine and Sir John Meldrum were issued with a Patent for the same area of land. This Patent also gave the Patentees the right to erect as many lighthouses that may be required within a 2 mile radius. The final clause in the Winterton Patent showed the importance of Royal Favouritism, *'For their true, faithful and acceptable service as being the first suitors to him for erecting lighthouses near Winterton and for other good causes and considerations.'* There is no record to show what these considerations were. [13]

Trinity House was told by the Patentees that it could continue with its light but an agreed lease would be necessary. The Corporation refused to consider the offer. To further insult the Elder Brethren, the Patentees were allowed to use the Corporation's newly built lighthouse free of charge until they had completed their own. Although a formal protest was sent to Sir Henry Yelverton by the Elders of Trinity House, only a short reply was received. In this letter the Attorney General stated that the King was guided by Divine Right and; if he agreed with the Privy Council's arrangement with the Corporation, it would be taking away his powers as monarch.

Private Owners, Smugglers and Wreckers.

Known as the *'Graveyard of Ships'*, the coastline around the Lizard headland would be the subject of a Patent involving James I. This particular Cornish area was caught up with the openly active smuggling and wrecking communities. Any private lighthouse owner who was likely to break these livelihoods of *'Custom and Descent'* would need to be someone well versed in these traditions. Sir John Killigrew was such a person.

Killigrew's family were well known in the early 17th century as smugglers and privateers. As landowner for Lizard Point he enlisted the help of his cousin, Lord Dorchester (*Ambassador to Holland*), to obtain a Patent for a lighthouse. In May 1619, James I authorised the Duke of Buckingham, a close friend of the King, to issue a Patent to Sir John Killigrew. The Duke of Buckingham signed this document in his capacity as Lord High Admiral of England. Killigrew was surprised to note that his Lizard Point Patent only gave him the right to collect a lighthouse levy from shipping on a voluntary basis. [13]

During the building of the Lizard Point lighthouse; around the summer of 1619, local inhabitants attacked the workforce and pulled down the partly completed tower. Killigrew was forced to employ a company of dragoons to protect his builders. The local community openly condemned the proposed lighthouse as they believed it would take away their livelihood from the rich pickings of winter shipwrecks.

In 1620 the Lizard light was first lit but the voluntary contributions for its upkeep failed to materialise. On several occasions Sir John Killigrew sent a group of his henchmen out in a cutter to intercept passing ships. Near the end of 1620 the Lizard light was extinguished. Two nights after Killigrew made this decision a fleet of ships coming up the English Channel nearly ran aground off the Lizard Point. Although the ships Masters paid the light levy, the matter reached the ears of King James. By the middle of 1621 the number of ships wrecked near the Lizard Point had become totally unacceptable. The following year, James I ordered the light to be relit. In 1623 the King ordered that '*a lighthouse should remain for all times on that part of the coast*' and extended the Patent for '*as long as Sir John Killigrew or his partner Thynne may live*'.

It is difficult to understand the motive of Sir John Killigrew for erecting the lighthouse on Lizard Point. On one hand he appeared to be protector of ships whilst on the other a smuggler, privateer and wrecker. When the Lizard light was unlit in 1627; for which no explanation can be found, Sir John Killigrew was accused of piracy after a silver bullion ship was wrecked near the Point. A report was made to the Lords of the Privy Council and to Lord Dorchester, that Sir John Killigrew had ordered his men to salvage the cargo and threatened to kill the ship's surviving crew. The Privy Council accepted Sir John Killigrew's explanation that he had acted under '*Custom and Descent*' and that the King had received his share of the cargo in the normal way. Sir John Killigrew died two years after his partner Thynne in 1630. Although a relative applied for the Patent, it was refused.

Strange Events at Spurn Point

A strange patent was issued to the Angell family in 1675, despite the fact that the land where the lighthouse was to be built belonged to Lord Dunbar. Land originally owned by the Angell family had been washed away by the sea. In 1609 two Angell brothers obtained the land known as Spurn Point, together with the fishing rights around its coast. In time the land was bequeathed to a Justinian Angell. Following numerous wrecks along this stretch of coastline he applied for a Patent to erect a lighthouse and enlisted the help of his cousin Joseph to obtain signatures from Shipowners and Merchants for the petition. However, Justinian Angell decided to build a lighthouse and to display a light before the petition was sent to the Lords of the Privy Council.

He then bribed members of Trinity House with £80 per year, disguising it as an annual subscription to the Corporation's Charities. Not surprisingly, the Corporation offered no objection. In November 1675, the Privy Council for Charles II issued a Patent for the Spurn Point lighthouse which was authorised Justinian Angell to collect by compulsory contribution '*one quarter penny per ton from all passing ships*.' These levies were to be collected at the vessels port of destination by the revenue officers. In 1678 the Patent was amended with the levy raised to a '*halfpenny per ton from English ships and one penny per ton from foreign*'. [6]

Justinian Angell died in 1680 and left the Spurn Point Patent and all its rights to his wife and son John, but by 1690 Lord Dunbar was waging war against the Angell family over the disputed land ownership. One night Dunbar sent his men to wreck the lighthouse and in the process they took the keeper prisoner. The matter went to the court of William III who ordered that the keeper should be released and the land returned to the Angell family. John Angell died in 1750 and his son, also John, assumed the management of the

Spurn light.

In 1751 the land agents for the Crown, were instructed by the Privy Council of George III to establish, once and for all, the ownership of Spurn Point. Whether John Angell bribed the land surveyors is not known but he managed to establish the land as his own. It is suggested in Trinity House papers that John Angell moved the land markers while the surveyors were at a local inn. [3]

Cromwell and Pepys

On the 17th March 1649, Oliver Cromwell abolished the monarchy and turned England into a Commonwealth. Later in that year he suspended the Trinity House Charter with disastrous results. Along with the Navy and Customs Officials, Trinity House was investigated with all Royalist sympathisers either sacked or forced to resign. The Master, Richard Crandley (1648-9), and the majority of Elders were amongst those removed. In their placed Cromwell set up an ill-informed and totally useless committee. [8]

Following the restoration of the monarchy, on the 8th May 1660, Charles II re-established Trinity House to its previous status. General Monk became the new Master and later the King conferred the title of Duke of Albermarle upon him for his services to the Crown.

Thanks to the diaries of Samuel Pepys (1633-1703) there are well documented records of this period. His involvement with the Navy office and Trinity House, soon put him in the position of a Younger Brother in 1662. He later became Master (1685-86) and drew up a new Charter which clearly laid out the duties of the Trinity House. Formally issued by James II, it was received by the Elders on 8th July 1685.

From the implementation of the James II Charter the serious business of erecting lighthouses began around England. Prior to this time Trinity House had been responsible for the building of only one lighthouse at Lowestoft. Other lights had been impeeded by succesive monarchs, who favoured the Private Owner. In turn Trinity House only received an attendance fee, for ensuring the lighthouses were properly maintained.

Now the pace increased and by 1695 there were 16 coastal lighthouses, which included Dungeness, Hunstanton, Orfordness, Lizard and Spurn Point. So dramatic was the building programme that by 1819 the number of substantial lighthouses had increased to 37.

Samuel Pepys; from a portrait by Kneller hanging in Magdelene College, Cambridge

Pilot Licensing

During the later part of 1687, the Corporation's activities widened even further as it gained the authority to examine potential pilots and to issue them with certified licences. Trinity House had always had an interest in pilotage, but formal powers to examine these pilots came after Pepys's visit to Spain in 1684. He had been impressed by the Spanish system of examination, adopted by the 'Casa de Contracion', a Spanish authority for the management of trade to the Indies. This examination board consisted of Don Miguel Zuero, the Master map-maker of Spain, the 'Piloto Mayor', a distinguished member of the 'Universidad de Mercantes' (College of Merchants) and six master pilots. Any aspiring pilots were publicly questioned on their knowledge of navigation and sea management with only the best achieving a certificate of competence to become pilots. This idea was readily accepted by James II and formally acknowledged in the 1685 Charter.

Trinity House was also authorised to fix its own rates of pilotage and more importantly, to examine Masters for the Navy. This part of the Charter came up against a great deal of opposition; especially from the 'land-based' politicians of the Admiralty Board, whose only thoughts were for lower overheads from sea-trade, no matter who piloted the ships.

On the 24th February 1696, Ambrose Marshall became the first recorded pilot to receive his licence. His documents, issued by Trinity House, allowed him to cover the area down the Thames as far as Gravesend.

Patronage and Press Gangs

Whilst in the position of Secretary to the Navy Commission (1683), Pepys had openly condemned the practice whereby senior Naval officers promoted their footmen and allowed them to become 'Gentlemen-Captains'. This term referred to anyone who had volunteered for a commission but was not a 'bred' or experienced seaman. Although these practices were also condemned by Admiral Sir William Booth, Admiral Sir John Berry, and Sir Henry Shere, the Admiralty; who had no senior Naval Commander on the Board, simply ignored the complaints. [15]

Not only did Berry, Booth and Shere condemn the practice of appointing 'Gentlemen - Captains', but so did the close friend of Lord Dartmouth and Admiral Sir Christopher Myngs. All believed that only those well versed in matters of the sea should be considered suitable to be Commanders of the King's fleet. This would only happen when 'true tarpaulins' (fully experienced mariners brought up with a life on the seas) became the only ones recognised for the positions of a Ship's Masters. Full authority for Trinity House to examine Masters for the Navy was given on the 25th September 1688, following an Act of Parliament which brought into operation the new rules which governed the selection of ship commanders and other ranks. [16]

Trinity House Elders were appointed Examiners for the Mathematical Scholars of Christ's Hospital. This powerful body of Master Mariners also had the power to appoint British Consuls in many overseas ports.

One of the Elders less publicised activities, was their authority to act as auxiliary press-gang officers. On a few occasions Trinity House overstepped the mark and forced the wrong people into service. On the 21st November 1685,it was ordered to provide labour for the PHOENIX which was due to sail on the next high tide. A member of the Younger Brethren obtained the services of the Master of the GLOBE and, along with Captain Gifford (the Commander of the PHOENIX), illegally pressed two customs officials and a butcher into service. It was stated at the time, that Captain Gifford was 'somewhat warmed with wine'. [16]

Affairs of lighthouses in Ireland and Scotland

The first recorded petition to establish privately owned lighthouses in Ireland, was made by Sir Robert Reading to the Privy Council of Charles II. Sir Robert was educated at Oxford and admitted to the Inner Temple in 1659. He later became a member of the Irish Parliament for Ratoath in 1662 and in the same year married Jane, the widow of Charles, 1st Earl of Mountrath. In 1665 he was granted a Letter-Patent to erect *'two lighthouses upon the hill of Howth; a lighthouse on the Isle of Magee, near Carrickfergus; another on the Old Head of Kinsale, near Barry Oge's Castle, in the harbour of Kinsale and a tower at Hook'*. After entering into a security for £5000 to pay for the upkeep and maintenance of the lighthouses, he was authorised to levy light dues from shipping. The Parliamentary documents state, *'One penny per ton on all inward and outward bound ships; boats;crayers and ketches'*, with foreign ships *'a charge of two pence per ton'*. The Patent also referred to fishing vessels belonging to any Irish Port. With these ships *'they shall pay only ten shillings a year, each at the respective seasons of fishing'*.

Regarding the unusual arrangement of dues being charged by the French Authorities, the Patent added: *'and ships belonging to the subjects of the King of France and trading to or sailing by any harbour in Ireland, shall pay the same due per ton coming in or out, as is charged upon Our ships trading to Bordeaux in France, towards the maintenance of the lighthouse of Cordouan, but such duty shall not be less than two pence per ton.'*

Although Sir Robert Reading's wife put up a £2600 surety for the erection of the lighthouses the project failed. Much of the financial difficulty arose from the refusal of numerous Masters and Shipowners to pay the required light dues. There was also the problem of Sir Robert's *'high lifestyle'*. To stay out of a debtors prison, Sir Robert surrendered his Patent, but in the form of a trust for his wife and himself, to Richard, Earl of Arran.

In 1668 the Isle of Magee lighthouse was abandoned, much to the concern of Irish shipowners and Merchants. Around the end of 1704, the Earl of Arran gave up the Patent to Customs Commissioners appointed by the Irish Parliament. This was the only Royal Letter-Patent issued to a private individual for a lighthouse in Ireland.

Soon after Sir Robert was issued with his Letter-Patent, the Merchants of Dublin Harbour petitioned the Irish Parliament for a much needed lighthouse in Dublin Bay. It would take nearly six years before Parliament granted permission, with a Letter-Patent issued for the construction of the Howth Bailey lighthouse. This structure was finally established in Dublin Bay in 1671.

In Ireland, overseas trading during the 17th century was relatively small and mostly localised between Dublin and Liverpool. As a consequence, there were very few Irish lighthouses until the restoration of the monarchy in 1660. In 1704 Queen Anne transferred management of all Irish lighthouses to a group of men classed in name only as *'Commissioners'*. It is believed this referred to senior officials in the Customs and Harbour Board of Dublin. From this time onward, there were no privately owned lighthouses in Ireland.

As the sea trade increased in Dublin Bay, so did the population. Soon Dublin was regarded as the second largest port in the British Isles. As more overseas trading came to the port, the need for suitable navigational lights became a priority. A form of Irish rutter dated 1749 and called the *'Compleat Irish Coaster'*, included a surveyors report that went into detail about the quality of Ireland's major lighthouses. It stated that there were only three lighthouses: Hook, Howth Bailey and Old Kinsale, with only one lightvessel in Dublin Bay that was established in 1739.

The oldest operational lighthouse in Ireland.
Hook Head, Co. Wexford.

Ballast Board of Dublin

One significant approach towards Irish lights, came with a Letter-Patent issued to James Palmer in 1740. This document gave him the authority to erect and manage all water marks and buoys in Dublin bay. It is also understood that this authority included the harbour lights as well, which at the time caused a great deal of bad feeling from the local Harbour Board.

In 1767 an Act of Parliament transferred the management of all Irish lights to the Commissioners of Barracks. This group of predominantly Army or Navy officers, became the first recognised authority for the Irish lights.

However, the Customs board strongly objected to this arrangement and stated that its officers were better placed to manage the lights. It also stated that its services would be far more economical and effective. The objections were considered logical by the Irish Parliament, which passed another Act to transfer the management of lights to the Customs officials. Just to confuse the issue, a previous Act of Parliament had formed the Commissioners of the Irish Lights into a Corporate body, but this venerable group of Master Mariners were looked upon only as the '*Corporation for Preserving and Improving the Port of Dublin*'.

Within four years of the Customs Board taking over the management of

23

the Irish lights, it had increased the number of lighthouses to eight. But the promised economical administration failed to materialise. When an official audit was ordered by the Irish Parliament there were so many discrepancies and queries over misappropriation of funds, that many of the senior Customs Officials were sacked. Following this scandal an Act of Parliament in 1810 made the Port of Dublin Authorities the sole responsible body for maintaining and managing the Irish lights. Although it was known officially as the Dublin Port Authority, it was better known to the shipping fraternity as the Ballast Board.

The 1810 Act of Parliament also brought fourteen lighthouses under the control of the Corporation, namely South Rock, Old Head, two lights in Wicklow, Copeland Fort, Charlesfort and Old Head of Kinsale, the latter often being called Barry Oge's Castle.

Slow Growth in Scotland

Originally there seemed to be little demand for lighthouses in Scotland, supposedly based on the small amount of shipping. This situation remained unaltered right up to the 18th century. The following extract is typical of contemporary writings: '*To understand the need for lighthouses along the Scottish coastline, not only must the terrain be considered, but sea trade and commerce. If the existing trade of goods can be transported overland or be self supporting within its own borders economically the need for a light does not arise.*'

As late as the mid 1700's, Scotland had only one lighthouse worthy of the name, built on the Isle of May in the Firth of Forth by the partnership of John Cunningham of Barnes and James Maxwell of Innerwick following a Letter-Patent issued by Charles I in 1635. The lease was for nineteen years at a rental of one thousand pounds '*in coin of this realm*' - actually £84 sterling. This Patent was the only Royal authorisation given to private individuals in Scotland. Consisting of a crude pile of rocks with a coal burning brazier on top, it was frequently criticised as being very poorly visible, a common complaint with coal fires throughout the history of lighthouses.

The lighthouse at Isle of May was reported in 1799 to burn as much as 400 tons of coal each year and on one stormy night alone it used 3 tons. During windy conditions the light frequently lit up the land instead of the sea. In 1810, believing a nearby lime kiln fire to be the Isle of May light, the Captains of HMS NYMPHEN and HMS PALLAS misread the light with both vessels wrecked and the loss of nearly all their crews.

In 1656, Oliver Cromwell commissioned Thomas Tucker to carry out a survey for the purpose of recording the extent of sea trade in Scotland. His report focussed on the Port of Glasgow, a small market town, 22 miles from the sea, with a medieval university and a Cathedral. In the report his comments stated, '*it is chequered and kept under* (low trading levels) *by the shallowness of her river, so that no vessels of any burden can come nearer up than fourteen miles, where they must unlade and send up their timber and Norway trade in rafts or floaties; and all other commodities by three or four tons of goods at a time.*'

From these early beginnings no-one would have thought that dredging and widening the River Clyde could transform this market town into the crowded smoky industrial city it is today. Nor that the river would be capable of carrying some of the World's largest vessels. Although some work was done during the years following the Tucker report, the same system of trading continued for nearly 100 years when, in 1750 the dredging work was officially put into operation. By 1755, navigational lights did appear along the river banks, but only in the form of small lanterns that guided the ships through the Clyde and into the rapidly expanding Port of Glasgow. By 1700 there were still only two lighthouses in Scotland, the Isle of May and the lights at Buddoness built by Trinity House of Dundee.

Up to 1755 there was no recognised Lighthouse Authority in Scotland. Then, in January 1755, the Glasgow Town Council instigated a Bill for presentation to the Unionist Parliament in England which aimed to establish a lighthouse on Little Cumbrae Island and to remove various obstacles and shoals from the lower reaches of the River Clyde. The original application stated that the Council's intention was to set up *'beacons and marks for evicting such dangers, by making other necessary works . . the Navigation in the said Firth and River Clyde will be rendered more safe and commodious.'*

The Bill was presented to Parliament at the beginning of 1756, in March the matter had been debated and by April, the Act had been given Royal Assent.

In 1959 Stevenson wrote *'This measure, obtained so speedily at a cost of some £200, was one of the chief practical steps taken to develop Glasgow,'* Included in the Act was the Crown Authority to collect *'one penny sterling per ton'* from every British ship (excluding His Majesty's warships) and *'two pence sterling per ton'* from foreign vessels which passed the lights.

A charge could also be levied from any outward bound British ship or homeward destined foreign vessel. This was rated at *'a sum not exceeding one penny and a half sterling per ton'* for British ships and *'three pence sterling per ton'* from foreign vessels. [13]

A Board of Trustees mainly consisting of nominees of the Glasgow Town Council was set up to implement this new Act of Parliament. When the Little Cumbrae light dues started to accumulate, much of the money was wrongly used to dredge and widen the upper reaches of the River Clyde and for further navigational lights entering the Port of Glasgow. [13]

Commissioners of Irish & Northern Lights

The prime turning point in defining the rights of Trinity House of Deptford occurred in 1786, with the passing of the George III Act of Parliament. This Act laid out the powers of the Corporation, as well as creating two new Lighthouse Authorities; The Commissioners of Irish Lights and Commissioners for the Northern Lights. [17]

At last Ireland would be able to administer its own affairs, relating to its lights, with Scotland in a similar position but with the responsibility of the Isle of Man. However it would be a few years later, before the Commissioners for the Northern Lights actually became responsible for the lighthouses on the Isle of Man. Trinity House of Deptford would administer the domain of England and Wales, the Channel Islands and the Isles of Scilly.

Originally the constitution for the newly formed Irish Lighthouse Board, was 21, which included the Lord Mayor and High Sheriff of Dublin, three Alderman elected by the Municipal Corporation of Dublin each year and 17 co-opted members filled by the Board when vacancies occurred.

Those holding office in the Northern Lighthouse Board, comprised of the following:- *The Lord Advocate and Solicitor for Scotland, The Lords Provost of Edinburgh, Glasgow, Aberdeen and Inverness; the Sheriff Principals of Glasgow and Strathkelvin, North Strathclyde, Tayside, Central and Fife, Grampian, Highlands and Islands, Dumfries and Galloway and the Lothians and Borders.*

With its new authority, the Commissioners were awarded a Letter-Patent which gave them the permission to erect four new lighthouses. Dated the 25th November 1787, the actual Patent document read:- '*Whereas by an Act passed in the Twenty sixth year of his present Majesty's Reign, intituled, an Act for erecting certain Light-Houses in the Northern Parts of Great Britain, the Commissioners therein named were enabled, for the Security of Navigation and Fisheries, to erect four Light-Houses in the Northern parts of Great Britain; One at Kinnaird's Head, in the County of Aberdeen; One in the Island of North Ranilsha, in the Orkneys; One on the Point of Scalpa, in the Herries; and a fourth in the Mull of Kintyre; and from and after that time such Light-Houses should be finished, in such a manner as to have proper Lights or Signals put up therein, to demand, collect, receive and take, from Masters and Owners of every British Ship or Decked vessel, navigated according to Law, passing any of the said Light-Houses, a sum not exceeding One Penny Sterling per Ton; and for every foreign Ship, or Decked Vessell, passing as aforesaid, a Sum not exceeding Two-pence Sterling per Ton.*' [17] These lighthouses are better known today as Eilean Glas (Point of Scalpa); North Ronaldsay (Island of North Ranilsha), with Kinnaird's Head and the Mull of Kintyre.

Today there are nominees from the Isle of Man, although originally the Commissioners of the Northern Lights, did not, in practice however, take on the responsibility of the Isle of Man lights until 1817.

Private ownership and slow progress on the Isle of Man.

On the 30th December 1771, John Quayle; for the Corporation of Trinity House of Deptford, wrote to the Duke of Atholl; the Lord Governor of the Isle of Man, to inform him that a Mr. Ludwidge had taken up a lease for part of Langness on the peninsula Island of St. Michael's.

This Island's location placed it at the most south easterly end of the Isle of Man, which prompted Mr. Ludwige to make proposals to Shipowners and Merchants at Whitehaven and Workington, for the erection of a much needed lighthouse. His intentions also indicated that the Langness lighthouse would be built and managed by him, as a private venture, but only if the Trade agreed to a levy of '*one penny per ton*' from shipping for its upkeep, when passing his light.

Numerous Shipowners and Masters supported Ludwige's proposals, however, the lucrative shipping from Liverpool did not. These well organised Liverpool Shipowners and Masters stated that the proposed light would not cover the area which was needed; around the dangerous waters of the Calf of Man and Spanish Head. Also these Shipowners were becoming dissolutioned with Private owners, because of their varied levies and often poorly managed lights. Liverpool Shipowners favoured a similar system which was in operation in their own Port, that was being successfully managed by the Board of Dock Trustees.

This disagreement relating to the Langeness light continued, with the Liverpool Shipowners formally objecting to every new proposal put forward by Mr. Ludwidge. The stalemate seemed unbreakable, with Trinity House of Deptford insisting they would only act if the project had the backing of the majority of Shipowners. It was also important that this backing was unanimous, because once the light was established, it would be the Shipowners who contributed towards its upkeep.

After many years of inaction, the Commissioners of the Northern Lights began to assert their influence and wrote to the Duke of Atholl. In their letter, dated the 2nd May 1815, they informed the Duke that their attention had been drawn repeatedly to the dangerous hazards which shipping was being exposed to around the extreme points of the Isle of Man. They also stated they were prepared to apply for an Act of Parliament to remedy the problem.

A further two years passed before any real action was taken over the Isle of Man Lights, until finally, a letter dated 15th January 1817, was sent by Sir William Rae, on behalf of the Commissioners of the Northern Lights, to the Duke of Atholl. In his letter, Sir William Rae enquired about the rates of compensation that would be necessary for the acquisition of ten acres of land. However, the Commissioners were surprised to receive the Duke's reply, which stated a further £50 per year would be required on top of the ground rent; which had to be paid to the lessee of the Calf of Man, because he would no longer have the exclusive right of use of the land.

The Commissioners considered the claim for compensation and decided to erect a harbour at the Calf of Man, which they knew would be beneficial to the business of the lessee. It is clear from the documents of the Northern Lighthouse Board, that they considered every reasonable demand especially if it was cost effective. They also realised that it would be more expensive to place the matter before Parliament, where a jury could; under an Act, fix a suitable rent. These particular points were mentioned in the correspondence to the Duke of Atholl, in which the Commissioners commented that they trusted that this action would not be necessary and hopefully *'with his Grace's influence, the lessee could be persuaded to accept the offer.'*

Apparently the Duke of Atholl must have finalised the deal relating to the Calf of man, because on the 7th June 1817, the Commissioners sent an acceptance notification that they were prepared to agree payment of *'ten pounds'* a year quit rent with the understanding that the Duke satisfied all claims that might be made by his tenant.

After a period of nearly 40 years, the final compensation document was agreed, but sadly, not before numerous vessels and their crews were lost off the Isle of Man. Certain records held by the Northern Lighthouse Board clearly note the survey reports on the Calf of Man, which had been supplied by its Engineer-in-Chief, Robert Stevenson. With this preliminary work already carried out, it took only ten months for the erection of the lighthouse, which was officially lit for the first time on the night of the 1st February 1818. [18]

Costly end to Private Ownership of Lights - England & Wales

In England and Wales, private ownership of lighthouses remained in existence until 1836. Although there were only about 10 such stations; with the major portion of the lighthouses already under the jurisdiction of Trinity House of Deptford, it was necessary for the Corporation to petition Parliament for an Act which would authorise the taking over of these private lights. Trinity House minute books for this period, clearly show the confused state of light levies around the early part of the 19th century and the pressure that was being applied by the Shipowners and Masters, for the unification of these dues and a centralised management.

Most of the complaints from Shipowners referred to the multi-payment system, whereby a vessel was charged for every light that it passed. Not only was this a financial burden, but the rates of dues varied from one light to the next. There were even numerous representations made to the Attorney General by the lighthouse owners, because of the excessive commission charge of 20% being deducted from the levies that the Customs officials collected. Although in some instances private agents were authorised by the owners to collect the light dues, the majority of these levies were the domain of the Customs officials. At one time some of these officials were considered to be the highest paid Crown Officers in Britain. Because of these problems, Trinity House of Deptford petitioned Parliament for the need to centralise the lighthouse management and ownership in England and Wales and to bring about a necessary reform on the system of light dues.

In 1834 a Select Parliamentary Commission was set up to enquire into the management of private lighthouses and the levies that their owners were authorised to collect. The Commission's chairman, Joseph Hume MP, became the main proposer of lighthouse management reform and the abolishment of private or leased lights. By 1836 an Act of Parliament made all the lighthouses in England and Wales, the sole responsibility of Trinity House of Deptford. [19] Further clauses were added to this Act, which gave Trinity House the power to purchase, by compulsory order, all privately owned lights. Of the remaining ten private lighthouses, three were designated to be under a valid Board of Trustees or by a Harbour Authority, such as Mumbles lighthouse near Swansea. Four other lighthouses were classed as being in '*Perpetuity*', which would require a further Act of Parliament to resolve the problem. [20]

The easiest private lighthouses to be taken over, were two which had designated leases. Among these was the Longships, off Land's End in Cornwall which had a 9½ year lease remaining, that was held by Henry P. Smith. The compensation for this lighthouse amounted to £40,696. Dungeness lighthouse was also under a lease, with 12 years and 175 days remaining to run. The compensation to its lessee, Thomas W. Coke, was £20,954.

Those which were '*In Perpetuity*' were clarified by an Act of Parliament, to have 23½ years left on their Patents. The official Parliamentary records do not show how the calculation for the remaining years was reached. The Tynemouth light, owned by Thomas Thorpe-Fowke, cost trinity House £124,678. Another '*Perpetual*' light was Spurn Point. The Angell Trustees originally contested the compensation offered of £300,510, but an agreement was finally accepted by J.B.B. Angell, of £309,531. [20]

Not all the private owners were prepared to accept the stipulated compensation, with the matter having to be settled by a jury. The Smalls lighthouse, another classed as '*In Perpetuity*' still had 41 years left from its original agreement. Its owners, the Rev. A.B. Buchannan (*the grandson of the original owner, John Phillips*) and his wife, with Thomas P. Clarke their partner, refused to accept the offer of £180,500. They provided the court with documentary proof, that over the previous 13 years the net profits for the light had increased by £4395 per year. Therefore the offer from Trinity House was unjust. The jury set the award of compensation at £170,468. The original lease for the Smalls lighthouse was due for renewal on the 25th March 1877. [20]

In each case of compensation, the calculations were always based upon the previous 5 years net profits. Even then it clearly shows the money which the private speculator was making, after the deduction of the much contested 20% commission charge by the Custom Officials. [20]

Skerries - The last Private lighthouse

As if in true form of holding records, the Skerries lighthouse was authorised by the last Letter-Patent issued by Queen Anne, on the 13th July 1714. So it seems only right that this lighthouse should become the last one to be purchased by Trinity House. However this was never intended to happen.

The Skerries became the most profitable lighthouse around England and Wales, from its first owner William Trench, to its last owner Morgan Jones II. When the 1836 Act of Parliament was implemented, Morgan Jones refused to accept any offer of compensation until the matter was officially addressed in court. He argued that the Corporation was not allowing for the increase in net profits after 1820. Over the period from 1836 to 1841, Morgan Jones was offered £260,000 then £350,000 and finally £399,500, by Trinity House. The Elder Brethren of the Corporation even asked Morgan Jones to stipulate a compensation figure based on his own estimates, but he refused.

By 1841 the matter had been addressed in three courts, until at last it was placed before the House of Lords. Morgan Jones stated that the decision of the Lords would be honoured and after a formal debate, the rates of net profit were set at £18,935 (approx) per year, which resulted in a total compensation payment of £444,984. Not only did the Skerries lay claim to previous records, it now proved to be the most expensive light that Trinity House had to buy. [20]

Triple Partnership v. Officialdom

By 1819, the Scottish Commissioners were responsible for 16 major lighthouses. When considering the atrocious weather conditions; the treacherous terrain on which these structures were erected and the difficulties of getting men and materials to site, can only be seen as exceptional.

In principle the 1786 Act of Parliament seemed workable and for 50 years most activities of the three Lighthouse Authorities ran smoothly. But in 1854, the Government amended the George III Act and transferred many of the responsibilities to the Harbour section of the Board of Trade.

Known as the Merchant Shipping Act 1854, it effectively split the Irish Lighthouse Board in two. The Port Authorities were given the title of '*Port of Dublin Corporation*', with the remaining Board becoming the '*Dublin Port and Docks Board*'. Each of these two bodies had identical constitutions and personnel, but very different functions. When the full division of the original Authority was completed in 1867, the Port of Dublin Corporation became the Commissioners of the Irish Lights. Trinity House remained in its original form, although much of the decision making with regards to erection of new lighthouses, was frustratingly effected by the Board of Trade. However, archive records of the Irish Lights, from around this period, clearly show that Trinity House still had a considerable influence over matters relating to lighthouses around Ireland. Yet most of the Parliamentary reports clearly state that this involvement was in an '*advisory capacity*'. In fact the Corporation was still using its power from the 1685 Charter, which demanded that the erection of any lights around the British Isles, was first sanctioned by the Brethren of Trinity House.

Although the Commissioners of the Northern lights came under the umbrella of the Board of Trade, following the implementation of the 1854 Act, they seemed to be the least affected. However the involvement of the Board of Trade was instrumental in delaying numerous lighthouse projects; seemingly because the powers to be felt it was necessary to investigate every objection to any proposals. In similar form for the other two Lighthouse Authorities, many of these delays amounted to nearly 10 years before the Board of Trade would sanction the finance for a proposed project. During this time the numbers of tragic shipping incidents escalated.

A report dated 1861 and provided by a Royal Commission that was appointed to investigate the affairs of the three Lighthouse Boards, clearly pointed out the confused organisation and needless expense that had occurred since the involvement of the Board of Trade. For the 402 lighthouses and other secondary lights, at that time, which were operational around the British Isles (including Ireland and Scotland), it needed 174 different local authorities to administer them. [1]

In 1880 the Board of Trade had completed its investigation into so called misuse of the funds from the Little Cumbrae Lighthouse dues and placed the lighthouses along the Clyde and four miles of the lower dredged river above Gourosk, under the jurisdiction of the Clyde Lighthouse Trustees. From that time this independent body became solely responsible for that stretch of waterway. When considering that the complaints from numerous Masters and Shipowners; about the Cumbrae funds being used to finance the dredging of the upper reaches of the Clyde, had begun 80 years earlier, it shows how quickly the Government had responded.

The Merchant Shipping Act of 1894 finally addressed the problems of the previous 40 years. It established the Commissioners of the Northern Lights as a Corporate Body, with their new authority designation for the '*Superintendence and Management of all buoys, beacons and lighthouses, throughout Scotland, its adjacent Islands and seas; including the Isle of Man.*' This Act also defined the responsibilities of the Commissioners of the Irish Lights and the Corporation of Trinity House. Its main directive was to remove many of the constraints on their actions, which had been caused by the involvement of the Board of Trade.

Trinity House of Deptford Properties

When the Corporation of Trinity House was first formed, its base was at Deptford, but it moved to Ratcliffe and then, around 1618, it moved to Stepney. But luck was not something that the Corporation could claim for the properties it used as headquarters. In 1660 the Corporation moved to Water Lane and six years later the building was destroyed during the Great Fire of London. Rebuilt in 1667, the building lasted only 47 years before it too burnt to the ground. Another property was built on the same piece of ground, but by 1793 it was in such a bad state that it was handed over to the Admiralty who decided the best answer was demolition.

Trinity House now stands on Tower Hill, in London a property designed and built in 1793 by one of its own architects, Samuel Wyatt. The exterior of the building clearly shows the character of the Corporation. Puff-cheeked cherubs adorn the facade and hold in their hands anchors, compasses and marine charts. The whole building is constructed from Portland stone with Doric columns and pilasters. There is a very large basement for storage of historical records; the ground floor contains offices whilst the upper floor consists of grand apartments where admission is by invitation only.

Once inside, a double staircase of solid Portland stone guides the way to a half landing with a wall decorated with a large oil painting. The staircase then branches left and right and meets on a central landing lined with ornaments, pictures and sculptures. The ceiling of the grand board room was painted in 1796 by the French artist Riguand and depicts the prosperity of England as it combines navigation with commerce.

To describe this wonderful ceiling is best started with the British Neptune who is advancing in triumph, surrounded by seahorses and attended by Tritons. In one hand he holds a trident and on his other arm is a shield of the United Kingdom. The regal march is protected by cannons and other items of war with unusual angels hovering around waving the Union Jack. On the other side of the ceiling Britannia sits on a rock receiving produce from many nations. Sea nymphs seem to be struggling under the weight of their presents as they approach the seated Britannia. There are also seamen laying out the fruits of commerce on the shores of England. To complete this extraordinary scene, children wave lit torches to represent the lights that encircle the English coastline.

Commerce and humanitarian scenes and the display of Neptune alongside Britannia would seem correct; but the depiction of cannons and other items of war might be considered out of place in a House founded for the well-being of seamen.

As the blitz of London increased in intensity during the Second World War, historical records, documents and irreplaceable paintings were packed into protective crates. These crates were due for transportation to a safe location on the 1st January 1941. But once more luck was not on the side of the Corporation, because on the night of the 29th December 1940, the Headquarters at Tower hill received a direct hit from an incendiary bomb which destroyed nearly all these treasures. When the war was over, Sir Albert Richardson, architect for the Corporation, was commissioned to restore the burnt-out Headquarters to its former glory. This work was completed in 1953 with the building officially re-opened by Queen Elizabeth II.

Through the years of political turmoil, fires and war, it is a sad fact that a very important part of the British lighthouse heritage has been lost. However, there is a slim ray of hope that some long forgotten documents may still survive. Many of the records and Charters were ordered to be handed over to the Government of Oliver Cromwell in 1650-51 and to this day, have never been returned. Pessimists say that it is doubtful that these documents still exist, because they were in the vaults of the House of Commons when the building was burnt down in 1834.

Lighthouse Builders - Eccentrics, Silk Merchants and Violin Makers

Many of the pre-Victorian lighthouses were not designed or constructed by people who would today be called civil engineers. The Eddystone Rock, for example, has a marvellous history which tells of an eccentric inventor, Henry Winstanley, who was the first person to tackle this formidable task. Yet his claim to fame was for the construction of a fully operational piped-water system and a water-closet which he built in London's Hyde Park during the summer of 1695. He enclosed his exhibition with a large tent and hundreds of inquisitive members of the public were charged '*sixpence*' for the privilege of seeing it in operation. Another of his inventions was a special guest chair. This seat had spring loaded arms that trapped any unsuspecting visitors as soon as they sat down. With this in mind it seems strange that anyone took Henry Winstanley seriously when he insisted he could construct a lighthouse on a reef in the English Channel, 14 miles offshore from Plymouth. The third tower to be built there was due to a silk merchant called John Rudyerd. Other lighthouses, such as the original towers erected on Hurst Point in Hampshire, were built on top of elm sleepers laid on a shingle bed. Surprisingly, neither of them fell down.

Another project at the Smalls lighthouse, 21 miles off St Davids's Head in Wales, was designed and built by Henry Whiteside a violin maker. The entrepreneur for the project was John Philips, a man whose business ventures had made him a virtual bankrupt, yet he convinced his creditors to back the venture. The original Smalls lighthouse was an octagon of wooden poles, topped by a cast iron hut, but it stayed in service for 85 years.

The Eddystone Influence

During the 18th century the building of harbours, breakwaters and lighthouses was looked upon as the domain of the civil engineer. This referred to any work carried out below ground or associated with bridges or contracts by the sea, but the roots of this important aspect of construction and design have a history which is relatively short. In 1662, Charles II founded the Royal Society and located its headquarters in London. This prestigious group consisted of eminent people who had made discoveries of a scientific nature, Doctors of Medicine, Physics and Mathematics. To be a Fellow of the Royal Society, FRS, was considered to be and still is, a scientists highest accolade. Sir Isaac Newton and Sir Robert Boyle were just two of its founder members. Sir Christopher Wren became the first person in architectural design to become a Fellow of the Royal Society, following the re-building of London after the ravages of the Great Fire in 1666.

Civil engineering as a profession did not really exist during the early part of the 17th century. Many historians have argued about who should be regarded as the '*Father of Engineers*'. Such names as Henry Winstanley, Henry Whiteside, John Rudyerd and John Smeaton have been mentioned. Following the destruction of John Rudyerd's Eddystone tower on the 2nd December 1755 when it was completely engulfed by fire, Robert Weston, the owner of the Eddystone lighthouse lease, contacted Lord Macclesfield, President of the Royal Society, for help in finding someone suitably qualified to build a new one. Smeaton was then finishing a scholarship sponsored by the Christopher Wren Foundation in the new and specialist aspect of construction, Civil Engineering. A formal recognition by the Society that the profession '*of Civil Engineer*' had begun, followed when Smeaton was appointed to build the new Eddystone lighthouse.

Difficult Access

Amongst the most difficult problems to overcome when constructing a lighthouse, were the remote and inaccessible locations. Choices for the building sites were always made to provide the maximum navigational benefit for the mariner. Of the Lighthouse Authorities in the British Isles, the task of the Commissioners of the Northern lights to build these structures around the coastline of Scotland were considered the most difficult. In November 1787, construction of the Mull of Kintyre lighthouse was complete except for installation of the light. The accessibility of the site combined with weather conditions were so bad, that the light remained unlit through the harsh winter because Thomas Smith, the Engineer in Chief, was unable to ship the small parts for assembly on site. Even in the summer of 1788 after the optic had been installed and with the Commissioners keen to start earning revenue,

Smith still refused to light the lamp until all the work on the keepers accommodation was finished. Though finished, the lighthouse had been unlit for eleven months.

The erection of the Bell Rock lighthouse off the Angus coast in Scotland was a magnificent feat of engineering, especially when considering that its base rock was barely visible at low tide and covered to a depth of 16ft (4.87m) during high water. What is more exceptional is the fact that this building work was started in 1807. Today technology has assisted in overcoming the problems of offshore engineering projects, but it is hard to imagine the conditions at the beginning of the 19th century. It is also noteworthy that the engineer for the Bell Rock lighthouse, Robert Stevenson, lived on board a floating light vessel along with his workforce throughout the entire project. During this period of lighthouse construction, many of the exceptional designers and engineers who built these towers around the British Isles, would never expect their workforce to be employed in conditions which they were not prepared to endure themselves.

Dangerous Locations

Similar conditions to those encountered by the Scottish lighthouse builders had to be overcome by the workforce of William Douglass when they erected the present Fastnet tower on the most southerly reef off the coast of Ireland.

Although the rock base for this lighthouse was above high water, it faced the full onslaught of the Atlantic Ocean. At times the force of the sea wave-washed the rock and after completion of this difficult project, the keepers were often stranded for weeks at a time in their living quarters.

Not all the projects attempted had a successful ending. The original Bishop Rock lighthouse, built on the most westerly reef of the Isles of Scilly, had been designed by James Walker and constructed by Nicholas Douglass and his son James. Its construction consisted of heavy cast iron stanchions anchored to the rock. After four years of back-breaking work, the project had been completed apart from installing the lantern and its light. On the night before the last stage of the contract was due to begin, the Isles of Scilly was struck by one of the worst storms in its history. It was two days before the Douglass workforce returned to the Bishop Rock, only to find the tower had been washed away by the power of the sea. All that remained were the stumps of the cast iron stanchions.

Lighthouse Engineers

Shared between the Commissioners of Irish Lights and the Corporation of Trinity House is the record that two brothers held the position of Engineer-in-Chief at the same time for both Lighthouse Authorities. Sir James Nicholas Douglass and his brother William were responsible for two thirds of the lighthouses around the British Isles.

In British lighthouse construction, the Commissioners of the Northern Lights have provided the highest standards of skill and ingenuity from many notable engineers and builders. In particular the Stevenson family, who designed and built no less than 81 lighthouses from 1808 to 1929, provides a fitting tribute to the work of this very important Lighthouse Authority. Amongst those men who have contributed towards the design and construction of Irish Lighthouses are the Engineers-in-Chief Cotton, Douglass, Halpin, Martin, Scott, Sloane and Smith. These exceptional men were responsible for the erection of 37 lighthouses between 1810 and 1969. Of these, Halpin was in office for the longest period, from 1810 to 1857 and was responsible for the construction of 23 lighthouses. Engineer-in-Chief Martin, was responsible for 6 lighthouses built between 1958 and 1969.

Another engineer who made a notable contribution to Irish lighthouse engineering was the blind engineer Alexander Mitchell; son of one of the Inspectors of Barracks, who invented a special screw pile which revolutionised the way in which lighthouses were sited on sandy seabeds and in river estuaries. His invention was used extensively, not just in Irish waters and around the British Isles, but in many unstable waterways around the world.

Royal Connections

Since the Charter from Henry VIII in 1514, Charters have been successively granted by James I (1604), Charles II (1672), James II (1685), George II (1730), Victoria (1871, 1894), George V (1910), and a Supplemental Charter from Elizabeth II in 1978. Prince William, Duke of Clarence, was the first member of the Royal family to be elected Master in 1829 and he became King William IV the following year. Prince Albert, Queen Victoria's Consort, was Master from 1852-61, and Prince Alfred, Duke of Edinburgh, held the office from 1866-94. He was succeeded by Prince George, Duke of York and later Prince of Wales, until he became King George V in 1910. Prince Arthur, Duke of Connaught, became Master from 1910 until 1941 and was succeeded by the Duke of Kent, the present Duke's father, tragically killed in action in 1942. His brother Prince Henry, Duke of Gloucester succeeded him and Prince Philip, Duke of Edinburgh, was elected Master in 1969 on retirement of the Duke of Gloucester. HRH The Prince of Wales and HRH the Duke of Gloucester are also Elder Brothers. In 1995 the Duke of Edinburgh was re-elected as the present Master of Trinity House.

Reform of Light Dues

In the late 1980s, pressure grew for a reform of the system of light dues which had remained essentially unaltered since 1894. Light dues were levied only on commercial shipping, large fishing vessels and pleasure craft over 20tons and collected by the Customs and Excise departments of both the UK and Ireland.

However, one of the major navigational aids during the late 20th century proved to be the Decca Navigator system, transferred to management of the General Lighthouse Authorities in 1987. Since it had always been a primary aim that aids to navigation should be paid for by their users, it seemed appropriate to extend the levy to smaller craft by means of a flat rate annual fee. After further consultation, the Government decided not to adopt the recommendation. In 1991 the voyage charge per ton was raised to 35p and in 1993 the responsibility for collection of dues for the UK and Ireland, was given to the Institute of Chartered Shipbrokers.

More About Trinity Houses

In 1992 the Trinity House of Newcastle celebrated the 500th anniversary of its acquisition of the land upon which its building today stands. It remains a licensing authority for Deep Sea Pilots and maintains buoyage in the vicinity of the Farne Islands. Perhaps the least well known of all the Trinity Houses is that of Scarborough, founded on 21st October 1602 with a Charter giving it charitable aims. In 1747, the Trinity House of Deptford took over its control until 1855 when it acquired independence once more. The Scarborough

Trinity House has continued to the present day, with a President, 2 Wardens and 15 Brethren.

International Lighthouse Authority

Today the basis of understanding for the need of maritime navigational lights has overcome the political barriers with the Corporations of England, Ireland and Scotland having a very close working relationship. On a broader scale, national lighthouse authorities of other countries have been meeting and collaborating for many years. One of the first co-ordinated meetings was at the Great Exhibition in London in 1851. In 1882, the Master of Trinity House; Prince Alfred, Duke of Edinburgh, chaired a conference which aimed to establish a uniform system of buoyage and in 1929 London was host to an International Lighthouse conference. In 1955 the decision was taken to establish a permanent organisation for the exchange of technical information, with the International Association of Lighthouse Authorities (IALA) being founded in 1957. Since then this organisation has co-ordinated navigational policy-making around the World with conferences held every five years.

Lighthouse Keepers - End of an Era

As the twentieth century draws to a close, so ends the long tradition of lighthouse keepers. It is not the arrival of the technological age, which is giving the apparent view that lighthouses are on the decline, because the need for these towers of light is acknowledged world-wide to be as great as it ever was. However the ability to automate the operational side of a lighthouse; with a means to control these systems, by radio or telemetry monitoring equipment; devised in the 1970's, has brought about the decline of the manual task. One major factor was the spiralling costs and economics dictating the only course of action.

Much has been written about the lights and their lore; the designers and builders have lauded their obvious talents, yet surprisingly very little has been said of the countless years of steadfast service given by the anonymous lighthouse keeper. There are some stories which will never be forgotten, with one of the earliest of the 94 year old keeper, Henry Hall, who accidentally swallowed molten lead whilst trying to extinguish a fire in the lantern of Rudyerd's Eddystone lighthouse. He was rescued, only to die a few days later, the first medically studied case of lead poisoning. There were other very old men in the lighthouse service; under easier circumstances, such as the 92 year old Edward Dalgleish at the Silloth station.

The U.K. can also be proud that its lighthouse service had the first coloured keeper called Mingo, who was responsible for the original Harwich lights.

There are heros and heroines, notable among them is William Darling and his daughter Grace, who rescued the survivors of the Forfarshire, near their Longstone lighthouse. Even children have been reported as being responsible for keeping a lighthouse operational. This particular event was part of the tales told by the keepers of the Longships lighthouse. They stated that Cornish wreckers kidnapped a little girl's father, to prevent him from tending to his lights. However she managed to keep the light lit during the absence of her father, by standing on a pile of books; including the family Bible, in order to reach the lamps. The second Longships lighthouse was witness to a tragic event, when a keeper fell to his death whilst cleaning the lantern glass.

Keepers have even tended their lights alone, after a fellow operative was taken seriously ill or died. This was tragically noted at the Smalls lighthouse when it was necessary for the keeper to put the body of his dead companion in a makeshift canvas bag and hang it outside of the tower. Not only was this a sad occasion, but the keeper could not be relieved for nearly two months after his normal tour of duty was over because of the attrocious weather conditions.

On another occasion a keeper at Godrevy Island was taken seriously ill, which forced his companion to signal to the mainland that help was needed. However, the weather prevented any attempt for taking the sick keeper off the Island for a further three days. Even after this time the remaining keeper stayed at his post alone and tended to the duties normally covered by a full team. This work also involved managing the fog bell mechanism as well as the light. He was finally relieved nearly 10 days later and on reaching the mainland was met by the local Mayor and treated as a hero. On lonely rock-based stations these acts of loyalty shows an exceptional devotion to duty. Other personnel have died because of war-time action, especially noted were the three keepers who were killed during a bombing raid at St. Catherine's lighthouse on the Isle of Wight, during the second World War.

Very little has been written to acknowledge how these keepers have acted as unofficial coastguards, something which is now greatly missed. Numerous lives have been saved because of the prompt actions of the keepers in bringing the rescue services into operation.

There are also mysteries which abound as at the Flannan Islands lighthouse in Scotland. In typical Mary Celeste form, three keepers vanished without a trace in 1900, supposedly lost during a storm. Various other speculations have been made, yet no proof or even a body has ever been found.

To many people lighthouse keepers are predominantly male, yet women have frequently played a major role by taking on the formal duties of their husbands. Always in addition to their responsibilities as mothers and housekeepers.

Loyalty to the Lighthouse Service was more than just a job it was a way of life, with many incidences of generations of family members following in their fathers footsteps.

In some cases the keepers did very strange things, such as one particular Irish keeper who detonated an explosive fog charge in a drain to clear a blocked toilet. The result was messy, yet resoundingly successful.

As time rolled on, firstly the land-based lighthouse keepers and their families were replaced by an individual attendant and his wife. These keepers had stood by as continual flow of improvements were made to every aspect of their responsibilities. Changes to all the equipment, lighting, optics, power supplies and fog signal operation, were finally taken over by the technological tide. These modern systems needed little attention, with major advances made in their reliability. The use of helicopters to relieve rock based lighthouses, was a mixed blessing. Not only did it take away the often dangerous relief by sea, but it winged in the equipment which incrementally turned rock lights into ghostly automatons. With telemetry remote control monitoring any fault could be quickly rectified, with helicopters airlifting engineers on to these sentinels in a matter of hours. On completion of these automation programmes the traditional keepers left their towers of light forever.

With all the various and often complicated duties which these keepers carried out, from coastguard watches, meteorlogical observations, remaining at their posts during atrocious weather conditions, having no where to hide during wartime in an undefended tower and assisting in rescue activities, the modesty of these people is summed up in a comment made by one of them. He was asked what he did at his lighthouse, to which he replied: '*I only kept the light lit.*'

Services Today

Apart from the automated lights, the three General Lighthouse Authorities are responsible for maintaining numerous lightvessels, light floats, beacons, radio and radar beacons, Decca Navigation stations and numerous buoys; many of which, have been under going a solar powered conversion programme. The majority of this work has been carried out by AB Pharos Marine Ltd., of Brentford, Middlesex.

Each of these Authorities have purpose built Tenders, which have been designed and constructed so they can venture into places where other ships would never attempt to go. Most of the time these vessels are involved with buoy work, which requires a very high degree of seamanship skill on the part of its Captain and the Able-seaman who have to jump off the ship in all weather conditions, to attach hoisting chains to errant units.

Trinity House has the THV MERMAID and the THV PATRICIA; the Irish Lighthouse Board has the ILT GRANUILE, with the Northern Lighthouse Board having the MV PHAROS. The name PHAROS has a special meaning to the Northern Lighthouse Board. Due to the dramatic increase in sea trade in 1799, Thomas Smith, the Commissioners Engineer-in-Chief, was unable to charter a suitable vessel for moving his men and equipment to the various lighthouse construction sites. The Board authorised Thomas Smith to purchase a sloop that was nearing completion in a Leith shipyard. This vessel would be the first Tender for the Commissioners of the Northern Lights, which Thomas Smith proudly named the PHAROS of LEITH.

M.V. Pharos photo by Burniston Studios Ltd. - supplied by Northern Lighthouse Board

37

T.H.V. Patricia photo by Fotolite 1/8752 - 1982 supplied by Trinity House

I.L.T. Granvile photo supplied by Commissioners of Irish Lights

In common with each of the General Lighthouse Authorities, they are financed from the Mercantile Fund (General Lighthouse Fund), by the UK Secretary of State for Transport. This fund is maintained directly from the light dues levied on shipping that uses the services these Corporations provide. It is important to note that none of the expenses for these Corporations comes from the taxpayers pocket.

Today the General Lighthouse Authorities are recognised officially by the Merchant Shipping Acts of 1894,1979 and 1988. From April 1993; and following the requirements of the Ports Act, light buoys and beacons, which are considered to meet the needs of only local navigation, were transferred to the control of the relevant Harbour Authorities.

Future Maritime Navigational Policy

A recent study was carried out for maritime aids to navigation, that will be required in the 21st Century. Broad consultations were held across the entire spectrum of the relevant International organisations, where it was agreed that the best future mix of navigational equipment would consist of:

1. Traditional visual aids
2. Shipborne radar systems assisted by racons and target enhancers;
3. Differential global positioning satellite system (DGPS) for accuracy to 10m;
4. A ground-based Long Range Navigation System (LORAN) to replace DECCA for accuracy up to 100m;
5. The US NAVASTAR satellite global positioning system for accuracy to 100m; improved GPS on a regional basis after 2003.

Even with Modern Technology

There is a poignant reminder which was expressed by an Elder Brother of Trinity House of Deptford during the late 19th century, when he responded to unfair criticisms made about lighthouses. A newspaper published an article which reported the comments of various shipowners, following a series of tragic shipping disasters around Cornwall. The Elder Brother said: '*lighthouses do not prevent ship wrecks, they only provide the mariner with the means to avoid dangers that they mark.*'

Even today, despite sophisticated satellite navigational systems and numerous technological maritime aids, shipping accidents still occur.

In March 1996 the SEA EMPRESS, ladened with thousands of tons of crude oil, ran aground at Milford Haven. The incident happened in broad daylight, with good visibility, fair weather conditions and under the gaze of the St. Ann's lighthouse. Keepers and their families had to be evacuated because of the toxic and potentially explosive fumes, that filled the air for miles around.

Although there was no loss of human life, the ecological effect on sea birds and marine life has yet to be calculated.

It is therefore pleasing to note a remark made by a Master of an ocean-going merchant ship. When asked how he felt about lighthouses he said: '*I have all the modern navigational equipment on board, but there is nothing more friendly and welcoming than the sight of a flashing lighthouse.*'

Reference Sources

1. Findley A.G. 'A Description and List of Lighthouses' 25th Ed. (1885)
2. From records held by the Lord Louis Museum, Isle of Wight.
3. Tait T.R., 'Early History of Lighthouses' Edinburgh (1902)
4. John Wormby, 'An account of the Corporation of Trinity House of Deptford Strond and of Sea Marks in General.' (1861)
5. Harris G.C. 'The Trinity House of Deptford. (1969)
6. Douglas B. Hague & Rosemary Christie, 'Lighthouses: Their Architecture, History and Archaeology'. (1975)
7. Public Record Office, London. Patent Rolls C82/388
8. Barrett C.R.B., 'The Trinity House of Deptford Strond. (1893)
9. Pepysian M/S. Misc. VII No. 1490,509.
10. Trinity House Charter, Public Record Office, London. Vol. f. 121. V
11. Select Committee Report on Trade, P328 (1822)
12. 13th Report of the Historical M/S Commission. app. IV, 166-71
13. Stevenson D. A., 'The World's Lighthouses Before 1820.' (1959)
14. Public Record Office. Charter Rolls James I (1604)
15. Pepysian M/S A196, Tangiers Papers.
16. Bryant, Arthur. 'Pepys' (1933)
17. Acts of Parliament. George III, 26/38, Sections 58/101.
18. Information supplied by the Northern Lighthouse Board (1985)
19. Act of Parliament, William IV, 6 & 7, C.79.
20. Parliamentary Papers, (1850-53), (1852-53) (295) XCVIII,519.
21. Historical Papers held by the Institution of Civil Engineers, London.
22. Williams, T. 'The Life of William Douglass.' (1920)
23. Information provided by the Association of Lighthouse Keepers.

Acknowledgements of Copyrights used in this publication.

Front Cover
Lower Left: The photo of the Bishop Rock lighthouse, was taken by F.E. Gibson and kindly supplied by the Corporation of Trinity House.
Centre: Reproduction of the Smalls lighthouse photograph, taken by Roger Dean, was authorised with the kind permission of Trinity House.
Upper Left: The Fastnet Rock lighthouse photo, was reproduced with the kind permission of its photographer, Finbarr O'Connell, Cork, Southern Ireland and originally appeared on the front page of the Sherkin Comment, Issue 21, 1996. It was supplied by the Commissioners of Irish Lights.
Lower and Upper Right: The photos of the Eddystone and Bell Rock lighthouses, were reproduced from the photographic library of Ken Trethewey.
Back Cover
This archive drawing has been reproduced with the kind permission of the Corporation of Trinity House, from a photo taken by Ken Trethewey. The original drawing was detailed by architect Samuel Wyatt, for the proposed first Longships lighthouse.

Notifications

The following details have been included in this publication, to acknowledge the assistance and support given by the various Lighthouse Authorities, Societies, Associations, Institutions, Historical Establishments and Governmental departments during the course of its research. It is only right that these sources of information are revealed, especially for other people who are carrying out their own enquiries, but were unable to find these organisations.

ASSOCIATION OF LIGHTHOUSE KEEPERS

The Secretary, Association of Lighthouse Keepers, 2 Queen's Cottages, Queen's Road, LYDD, Kent. TN29 9DN. The Association of Lighthouse Keepers was formed in 1988, by a group of serving and retired keepers. Its aim is to forge links with other Associations and Societies throughout the World; to act as an information centre; to expand its archives and to establish an International Museum and study centre.

Its close link with the International Lighthouse Authorities, makes this Association a focal point for information exchanges.

Membership is open to all enthusiasts, with members from all over the World.

TRINITY HOUSE NATIONAL LIGHTHOUSE CENTRE

Wharf Road, Penzance, Cornwall TR18 4BN, Tel 01736 60077.

This centre is located within the old Penzance depot on the site where the stone masonry was prepared for the Longships and Wolf Rock lighthouses. It houses, probably, the finest collection of lighthouse equipment and optical apparatus in the World. An audio-visual theatre traces the history of the first rock based lighthouses. A reconstructed living quarter, complete with its curved oak furniture, has been erected, which give a remarkable insight to the life of a rock based keeper. Tours are given most days by experienced and dedicated staff. A visit should not be missed.

SCOTLAND'S LIGHTHOUSE MUSEUM

Kinnaird Head, Fraserburgh, AB43 5DU, Tel: 01346 511022 Fax: 01346 511033

The purpose built museum sits across the headland, from Kinnaird Head lighthouse. A visit to the museum also includes a guided tour to the top of the building, which was one of the first lighthouses erected by the Commissioners of the Northern Lights.

Scotland's Lighthouse Museum has an extensive collection of photographs, lighthouse artifacts, a study centre and a comprehensive archives. Very helpful staff, who are extremely proud of their heritage. Well worth a visit.

COMMISSIONERS OF IRISH LIGHTS

The Inspector and Marine Superintendent, 16 Lower Pembrooke Street, Dublin 2, Ireland. Tel: 00353 166 24525

Established in 1786, the Commissioners of Irish Lights are responsible for all the lighthouses around the whole of Ireland. Service information is available, free of charge, on all its lighthouses, lightvessels, beacons and buoys. It has a comprehensive data-base on its lighthouse keepers and the people who erected these maritime navigational aids. Data is also available on ship wrecks within the confines of certain lighthouses.

Very humourous and extremely helpful staff.

NORTHERN LIGHTHOUSE BOARD

84 George Street, Edinburgh EH2 3DA Tel: 0131-226 7051
Fax No: 0131-220 2093

Limited records exist of shipwrecks or those stranded near lighthouses, manned at the time of the occurance. There is a comprehensive data-base relating to lighthouses, beacons, buoys and other services provided by the Northern Lighthouse Board.

Information packs are available free of charge, but if any specific request involves an outside agency, a nominal fee is charged. Very friendly and helpful staff, who are extremely proud of their lighthouse heritage.

TRINITY HOUSE LIGHTHOUSE SERVICE

Trinity House, Tower Hill, London, EC3N 4DH
Tel: 0171-480 6601 Fax: 0171-480 7662
Telex: 987526 (NAVAID G)

Any enquiries should be forwarded to the Records and Publications Officer, who will advise on the availability of the information required. Trinity House records include, position and dispersal of buoys, beacons and the lighthouses under the management of this Authority. However, many pre-second World War records were destroyed during a bombing raid in 1940, but those that survived are held by the Guildhall Library, in London.

Very helpful staff, who will undertake any enquiry. Initial request in writing.

GUILDHALL LIBRARY AND ART GALLERY

Guildhall Library, Aldermanbury, London EC2P 2EJ
Tel: 0171-332 1866 Fax: 0171-600 3384
Telex 265608 LONDON G

Apart from its comprehensive manuscripts and extensive library, it holds the surviving pre-war records of Trinity House and Lloyd's Register. These include brief details of ships, totally lost, published since 1890. A names index is also available from returns, post 1950. Board of Trade Inquiry Reports and sometimes additional information regarding a ship and its Master.

For best results with enquiries, write in first. Very professional and dedicated staff, with fast response to enquiries.

THE MARITIME SECTION

National Monuments Record Centre, Kemble Drive, Swindon SN2 2GZ Tel: 01793 414600 Fax: 01793 414606
E-mail: info@rchme.gov.uk

They gather and provide data on shipwrecks and other historical maritime sites, in England's coastal waters. Information is available to everyone, whether in person, by telephone, writing or E-Mailing the above address. They are always interested in maritime discoveries. The National Monuments Record Centre also holds the National Archives of archaeology, architecture and historical air photos of England; which include coastlines, piers, wreck sites and docks.

Fast response to enquiries, from friendly professionals.

HISTORIC SCOTLAND
Longmore House, Salisbury Place, Edinburgh, EH9 1SH
Licenses: 0131 668 8764
Recommendations: 0131 668 8650
Historic Scotland is best known as the Agency which opens over 300 archeological and historical properties to the public. It is also responsible for listed buildings, scheduled monuments and other related matters. It also has a maritime role, in operating the Protection of Wrecks Act 1973, in Scotland. If anyone wants to dive on a protected wreck, or underwater achaeological site of any sort, or recommend a wreck for protection, should contact this agency at its headquarters address stated above. Very helpful and friendly staff.

THE UNITED KINGDOM HYDROGRAPHIC OFFICE
Admiralty Way, Taunton, Somerset, TA1 2DN
Tel: +44(0)1823 337900 Fax: +44(0)1823 284077
This department maintains the wreck information for the Ministry of Defence and other Governmental agencies, it also offers a search facility for commercial and private enquiries. Any request for information must be addressed to the Wrecks Officer, which will receive an easy to follow guide how a search can be implemented. Small nominal fee is charged, but only according to requirements.

Very good value for money, provided by a down to earth and friendly staff. For a Government agency, the response time is exceptional.

THE NATIONAL TRUST
Souter Lighthouse, Coast Road, Whitburn,
Tyne and Wear SR6 79H
Tel: 0191 529 3161
In 1988 the Corporation of Trinity House decided to close the Souter Point Lighthouse, because of the decline in coastal shipping. At this time the National Trust agreed to purchase the station, which in turn added it to the preservation of the area that included the sea-bird sanctuary on the massive outcrop of Marsden Rock.

Although not an operational lighthouse in its former sense, Souter Point still continues to provide an aid to the mariner, through its automatic radio beacon.

Since 1871 when this lighthouse was first established, up to the present day, this station is open to the public, with many of its original machinery and equipment lovingly cared for by the numerous volunteers who upkeep the area.

A visit to this lighthouse, one of the first to be electrified, should not be missed.

THE ROYAL NATIONAL LIFEBOAT INSTITUTION
West Quay Road, Poole, Dorset BH15 1HZ
Tel: 01202 663000 Telex: 41328 Fax: 01202 663167

The Royal National Lifeboat Institution is a registered charity, which exists to save life at sea. It provides a 24 hour on call service, to cover the search and rescue requirements to a 50 mile limit from the coast of the United Kingdom and Republic of Ireland. Since its foundation in 1824, over 128,500 lives have been saved. There are 218 lifeboat stations, which are operated by volunteer crews, who are always ready to put their lives at risk to save others. In the majority of cases, they will aid people they have never met and probably never meet again.

The RNLI depends entirely on voluntary contributions for its income. For further information of how you can become a supporting member, contact the above address. There is also an exclusive children's club 'STORM FORCE'.

This publication and its companion booklet TO LIGHT THEIR WAY, have been produced to accompany the three series of individual stories about the lighthouses around England, Ireland, Scotland and Wales. To obtain your FREE LIST of these publications and details of OUR NO OBLIGATION TO BUY bookclub, send a SAE to B & T PUBLICATIONS, 10 Orchard Way, Highfield, SOUTHAMPTON. SO17 1RD (UK).

TO LIGHT THEIR WAY provides a detailed account of the various light sources, fuels, lanterns, reflectors and optical apparatus, fog warning systems, which have been employed in lighthouses. It also acknowledges those PEOPLE who invented, designed and manufactured this specialist equipment. Many archive drawings and pictorials have been included with this publication. This easy to read booklet gives the reader an insight to how the mariner utilises a maritime navigational light, its characteristics and who devised the system of flashing signals. The author of PHAROS: YESTERDAY, TODAY AND TOMORROW, Kenneth Sutton-Jones, has assisted in a major way, to ensure that the various technical details are correct. Included are the relative facts of these lighthouses present day operational mode. This publication is available from all bookshops, or direct from the publisher (POST FREE IN UK, EEC).

Trent Class Lifeboat - Photo by Rick Tomlinson (01703-458450) supplied by RNLI